General Theory of Law

Eduardo C. B. Bittar
Editor

General Theory of Law

New Challenges, Current Issues and Innovative Approaches

Springer

Editor
Eduardo C. B. Bittar
Faculty of Law
University of São Paulo
São Paulo, São Paulo, Brazil

ISBN 978-3-032-22516-0 ISBN 978-3-032-22517-7 (eBook)
https://doi.org/10.1007/978-3-032-22517-7

The original submitted manuscript has been translated into English. The translation was done using artificial intelligence. A subsequent revision was performed by the author(s) to further refine the work and to ensure that the translation is appropriate concerning content and scientific correctness. It may, however, read stylistically different from a conventional translation.

This Springer imprint is published by the registered company Springer Nature Switzerland AG
The registered company address is: Gewerbestrasse 11, 6330 Cham, Switzerland

Preface and Acknowledgements

The aim of the book *General Theory of Law: New Challenges, Current Issues and Innovative Approaches* is to bring together researchers who think about the current challenges facing the *General Theory of Law*. To the extent of the transformations of time and society, the *General Theory of Law* must be repositioned, in the face of the immense kaleidoscope of legal knowledge. A huge group of challenges arising from current times and the complexification of the functioning of legal-positive systems are posed to the *General Theory of Law*, which calls for a work of reflection to be installed on the role, function, actuality, and meaning of this area of knowledge of Law. This book should be considered a work of *Epistemology of Law*, *Theory of Law*, and *Science of Law*, because the knowledge of these areas is engaged. The aim of the book develops with a single focus, from start to finish. The research that is integrated into its content, however, seeks to maintain the autonomy of ideas that guides the intellectual production of each of the co-authors, which gives the work a line of work that respects the diversity of ideas and allows for the coexistence of different orientations in the same space of interlocution and scientific dialogue. The work therefore contains a unit and is divided into four chapters, each of which is written by a different author, and allows the reader to access historical reconstruction, conceptual categories, theoretical criticism, recent debates, and methodological discussions.

In the chapter *The historical genesis of the (General) Theory of Law, and beyond: origins, autonomy and methods*, Ana Margarida Simões Gaudêncio discusses and analyses the historical origins of the *General Theory of Law*. In her approach, she seeks to highlight the significance of the *General Theory of Law* locating it within modern history, with an emphasis on its position in the middle of the history of thought in the universe of Law. The chapter is dedicated to understanding the connection between its historical emergence and the search for rational autonomy, amidst a context of a transition between *Jusnaturalism* and *Juspositivism*. The chapter discusses the importance of the *General Theory of Law* to the consolidation of the *Science of Law*. Also, it seeks to discuss and analyse the method of Law, the modern concept of Law, and the process of historical affirmation of the *General Theory of Law*. At the end, the chapter is dedicated to developing, in addition to historical understanding, a critical evaluation of this legacy. This chapter also offers the reader, in its final topics, a broad overview of the most current panorama of *Legal Theory*, in its current pluralism, and its most significant *conceptual* and *theoretical-methodological* transformations.

In the chapter *The metascientific discourse of the General Theory of Law: the relationship between General Theory and Special Theories*, Eduardo C. B. Bittar discusses and analyses the *General Theory of Law* from a discursive approach, emphasising the importance of the reciprocal contribution between the *Semiotics of Law* and the *General Theory of Law*. In this interpellation, the text dialogues intensely with the contributions of Algirdas Julien Greimas, Peter Goodrich, Dominique Maingueneau, Maria Giulia Dondero, and Jerzy Wroblewski. Throughout its analysis, the chapter is dedicated to understanding the relationship between the *General Theory* and the *Special Theories*, which have emerged in the contemporary context, and which, gradually, are taking over the place of the *General Theories of Specialities* of the *Science of Law*. This point is placed at the centre of the analysis, insofar as what is observed is that the scientific universe in the field of Law is expanding, which has implied an increase in the branching of new fields of the *Science of Law*. In this context of transformations, it is debated whether the *General Theory of Law* is outdated and has lost its *discursive place*, in the face of the multiplication of the *General Theories of Specialities*. In fact, there is a repositioning, which needs to be analysed and exposed, of the *General Theory of Law* as a *federative science* of specialised legal knowledge. With this, the *reflexive force* and the *resolutive force* begin to coordinate more harmoniously, in the process of adapting the *General Theory of Law* to current challenges. This chapter is also dedicated to understanding the specific discursive nature of the *scientific enunciation* of the *General Theory of Law*, descending toward an exhaustive study of its specific qualities, which are (i.) *universal statements*; (ii.) *abstract statements*; (iii.) *empirical-analytical statements*; (iv.) *theoretical statements*; (v.) *rational and demonstrative statements*; (vi.) *complex statements*; (vii.) *unifying statements*; (viii.) *general statements*; (ix.) *polemic statements*; and (x.) *argumentative statements*.

In addition to these topics, the chapter also deals with the problem of the huge increase in circulation of data in a technodigital age, whose processing makes the task of the *jurist-Prometheus* the only one qualified to deal with the set of necessary information for the practical work of Law. In dialogue with the work by Ronald Dworkin, the concept of *jurist-Prometheus* is developed as an imaginary figure, but one that is, at the same time, a response to the contemporary tendency of delegating all knowledge to artificial intelligence (AI). With this, the *Science of Law* has been threatened by a farewell to reason. It is at this point that elaborating the criticism of *technocratic rationality* becomes necessary, with a view to valuing the *reflexive force* of the *General Theory of Law*, taking back its place, importance, and critical role in the dimensions of the concept of Law and its interconnections with the demands for justice and social emancipation. Throughout the analysis, there is a valuable dialogue with the contributions by Jürgen Habermas and António E. Pérez Luño on this subject. Taking this assessment into account, the aim is to stimulate a resumption of the understanding of the role that the *General Theory of Law* fulfils in our times, especially considering the tasks of a critical and situated understanding of the *General Theory of Law*, which is offered by the humanised and interdisciplinary approach of the theoretical model of the *Theory of Realistic Humanism*.

In the chapter *'New' questions concerning the experience of the Legal System and the problem of the sources of Law or the place and claims of an internal critical approach: going beyond the possibilities of a General Theory of Law*, José Manuel Aroso Linhares seeks to analyse and explore the relationship between two central points of the *Theory of Law*, on the one hand, the question of the *content of Law* (the issue of *Legal System*) as a legal system, and, on the other hand, the question of the *sources of Law* and its dimension of effective practical-social assimilation. The chapter explores the tension between the '*norm-ratio*' and the plural theory of sources. To this end, the chapter will have to dedicate itself to dealing with this relationship by a resumption of the theoretical legacy left by Savigny (*Gewohnheitsrecht*, *Gesetzesrecht*, *Juristenrecht*). In addition, the chapter will also explore the debate between Herbert L. A. Hart and Ronald Dworkin, focussing on the analysis of the concept of rule and multiple social sources. Furthermore, the article also questions the role of *inclusive positivism* and *exclusive positivism*, to thematise the multidimensionality of the legal system, with an emphasis on the idea of the plurality of the sources of Law. Finally, the chapter will focus on applying the theoretical model developed by A. C. Neves, from which it can derive the relationship between *system* and *sources* as one of *permanent tension* between *unity* and *plurality*. The chapter makes a valuable contribution to the search for a re-evaluation of this discussion, as it concludes by establishing an elevated role for *Legal Theory*, in view of its constant state of creative activity in the face of the dynamics of society.

In the chapter *Uncertainties and unpredictability of the legal system: the application of law under discussion*, Pierre Moor develops the theme of the relationship between Law and the universe of facts, in order to delve into a discussion about the dimension of the application and, with this, the challenges imposed by the insecurity that results from the analysis of the facts. On the one hand, if the legal system seeks legal security, on the other hand, the facts impose a state of insecurity that is continuous for the task of applying the Law. Thus, if the task of judicial analysis necessarily involves the understanding of the facts, this means that the *General Theory of Law* must be able to work on the way of knowing and appropriating the objects of the world. In this, it relies on the contributions of *Semiology*, under the influence of Ferdinand de Saussure, to develop well the narrative and argumentative understanding of the tasks of concretisation in the field of Law. Within it, Pierre Moor traces original analyses, as well as dialogue with authors like Niklas Luhmann, Umberto Eco, and Chaïm Perelman. The author also provides us with numerous concrete cases and examples drawn from practice, which give a technical dimension for understanding the challenges of Law. In this sense, the chapter will dedicate itself to understanding the dimension of the application of Law, in other words, the moment in which practical rationality is placed in question, functioning as a mechanism of empirical reality put into discussion. In conclusive terms, the chapter points to the idea that unpredictability and indeterminacy play a part in the practical tasks of Law, despite the incessant search for accuracy and precision. In this, Law is built between repetition and imagination, something which not even the adoption of algorithms by artificial intelligence can completely overcome. For this reason, when dealing with these phenomena, the judge absorbs the factual and legal dynamics, transforming them by abduction in judgements capable of offering credible solutions to concrete cases, doing so in a reasoned and justified manner, in order to make an adaptation between the dynamics of the legal system and the dynamics specific to society possible.

After this overview of the book, it must be said that this book would not have been possible without having had the immense support, interest, and dedication of *SPRINGER Publishing House* teams, to whose invitation all the researchers sought to accomplish with great enthusiasm and enormous gratitude. The book project has been maturing over the last 5 years (2021–2026), until it came off the drawing board, to be effectively written, counting on the tenacity of the researchers involved, over the last 2 years (2024–2025). This is the occasion to dedicate and record thanks to Karolina Araújo Martino, an editor with a bold vision for the area of Law. The organiser expresses his thanks to Ana M. S. Gaudêncio, José M. A. Linhares, and Pierre Moor, for the readiness with which they joined the project, and for an intellectual collaboration that has been nurturing an effective and very stimulating intellectual exchange over the years. This immediate and spontaneous affiliation allowed the productions of Portugal (*University of Coimbra*), Brazil (*University of São Paulo*), and Switzerland (*University of Lausanne*) to cross paths, so that together, they could incorporate a single and cohesive volume entirely and exclusively dedicated to the *General Theory of Law* and its current problems. The organiser also mentions CNPq, for the 1-B *Productivity Research Grant*, without which this project would not have been possible.

São Paulo, Brazil
November 3, 2025

Eduardo C. B. Bittar

Contents

The Historical Genesis of the *(General) Theory of Law*, and Beyond: Origins, Autonomy, and Methods

Ana Margarida Simões Gaudêncio

Abstract The present chapter intends to explore the genesis of the Theory of Law, starting from the meaning of General Theory of Law, within the internal History of Modernity, and emphasizing its relevance to the global History of Legal Thinking. It will involve an approach to the historical origins, rational autonomy and method of Legal Theory, concerning the transition from the period of predominance of Jusnaturalism to Juspositivism, and the consolidation of the Science of Law. Therefore, the foundational role of Legal Theory within the Modern concept of Law is exposed, concerning the rational links between Law and Legal Thinking. And, consequently, a critical approach to the subsequent developments points out the overcoming connections within Legal Theory.

1 *Legal Positivism* and the Origins of *Legal Theory*

The present chapter explores the genesis and development of the *Theory of Law*, starting from the meaning of *General Theory of Law*, within the internal history of Modernity, and stressing its relevance to the global history of *Legal Thinking*. Emphasizing the relevance of the split that has occurred since at least Modernity, in the context of Western civilization, the culturally and historically designed *General Theory of Law* will be exposed considering the inevitability of the long-term influence of various civilizational constructions, as a remote manifestation of diverse current meanings of *Legal Theory*.

Such an approach will require a return to the historical origins, the rational autonomy and the method assumed by that *(General) Legal Theory*, concerning the transition from the period of predominance of *Jus-Naturalism* to *Jus-Positivism*, and the consolidation of the idea of *Science of Law*. Therefore, the foundational role of

A. M. S. Gaudêncio (✉)
University of Coimbra Institute for Legal Research (UCILeR), Faculty of Law, University of Coimbra, Coimbra, Portugal
e-mail: anagaude@fd.uc.pt

E. C. B. Bittar (ed.), *General Theory of Law*,
https://doi.org/10.1007/978-3-032-22517-7_1

Legal Theory within the Modern concept of Law is explored, concerning the rational links between Law and *Legal Thinking*. And, consequently, a critical approach of the posterior developments points out the overcoming connections within *Legal Theory*, for, though far from the formalist discourses of the *General Theories of Law* that dominated *Legal Thinking* in the nineteenth century, the discussion between *Positivism* and *Non-positivism* assumes nowadays a crucial place, while discussing the specific foundations of law, among specific sense(s) and content(s) of *moral(s)*, or *morality(ies)*.

1.1 The Historical Construction of **Legal Theory** *as a Reflection of Modern* **History**

Contemporarily, the significances of *Legal Positivism*, in diverse forms, emerge from the discussion concerning the connection between Law and morals/morality, on the three main fields of *Legal Theory*, the realization of law and legislation,[1] much beyond the historical references of French and German Positivisms, on the one hand, and English and American Positivisms, on the other hand.

On its turn, *Legal Theory* expresses a very broad concept, meaning the *Theory of Law* and *Jurisprudence* in several ways and contexts, and, therefore, expressing the abstract construction of *Legal Thinking* toward law, both formally—in formalist and positivist proposals—and substantially—in natural law founded and other axiological proposals. From the political point of view, *Legal Positivisms* may assume several different positions–from which some must be stressed as, mainly, the following: *Liberal Positivisms*, *Neoliberal Positivisms*, Post-Liberal Positivisms.

From the scientific point of view, the several different presentations of *Positivist* approaches to law require a deep analysis of their origins, rational structures, and *modus operandi*. The definition of *the Legal Positivism* would represent, therefore, an unbearable intention and an impossible task to accomplish, because there are diverse concepts of *Legal Positivism* and, so, several different *Legal Positivisms*.

The remote origins of *Legal Theory* may, partially, be identified in the Middle Ages, and with deep roots in Roman Law.[2] The concept of Law was then mainly understood, concerning its foundation, as a normatively binding expression whose underpinnings would be established by an idea of natural law, and whose structure and content would consist in textual norms—both in the Continental and in the Anglo-Saxon Europe—though, with must deeper influence of Roman Law in the former than in the latter.[3]

[1] Scarpelli (1965), pp. 131–134.

[2] *See* Schultz (1953).

[3] *See* Gilissen (1979); Wieacker (1952), pp. 31.

Modernity brought a paradigm change in law's foundations, in legal thinking and in legal language,[4] exposing the notion of natural law to the development of an anthropocentric human perception and rationality. The Renaissance, Humanism, and the Reformation had already brought about profound changes in humankind's image of itself and of the world. Anthropocentrism is a fundamental step toward the autonomy of human reason in relation to God.[5] On the other hand, the crisis of the *ius commune*—and the concomitant discussion on the principle of authority—, the affirmation of individualism, and the ideal of stabilization, standardization, and rationalization, of the law, determined the concretization of rationalist natural law theories into codification—with the respective establishment of an order that could turn the dictates of *recta ratio* into positive and certain norms, an Enlightenment legacy.[6]

Rationalist Natural Law Scholars—such as Grotius,[7] Pufendorf,[8] Thomasius,[9] Wolff,[10] and several others—, adopting the model of empirical–analytical sciences, according to which the universe is governed by natural, universal, and necessary laws, sought to construct a system of norms deducible from rational, universal, and immutable principles of natural law, norms that would therefore constitute a rational order.[11] Those authors, assuming the *modern rationality*, intend to construct, based on empirical evidence resulting from the observation of nature, systems of immutable principles of *Natural Law*.[12] Then, from Jean-Jacques Rousseau,[13] and, mostly, from Immanuel Kant, *Natural Law* is disconnected from empirical observation and perception. In Kant's view, *Natural Law* becomes a pure a priori form, as a deontological determination of legal validity through human reason.[14] Such a foundation positions the positive (human) law and the natural (rational) law as two different systems, presupposing each other, mostly exposed through legislatives statutes. Modern-Enlightenment legal thinking emerged as an assertion of a new perspective on *Legal Thinking*, as well as a new foundation for law. *Natural Law* also emerged as a superior law, a model for positive law, but now founded on human reason, abandoning any metaphysical foundation. This gave rise to a new sense of Law and, as an expression of this, of *Legal Thinking*.[15]

---

[4] Luban (1997).

[5] *See* Marques (2003), pp. 79–110, 360, 381–383.

[6] On the causes and consequences of the *ius commune* crisis, see Marques (1986), pp. 43–50; Marques (2003) pp. 355, 362. *See* also Fassò (1970), pp. 13–14.

[7] Grotius (1625).

[8] Pufendorf (1672).

[9] Thomasius (1705).

[10] Wolff (1750).

[11] Marques (2003), p. 367.

[12] Marques (2003), pp. 367–368; Neves (1998–1999a), pp. 73–74; Truyol y Serra (1954), pp. 58–81.

[13] Rousseau (1762).

[14] Kant (1788, 1797–1798); Marques (2003), p. 445.

[15] *See* Marques (2003), pp. 365–421; Marques (1986), pp. 19–22. *See* also Neves (1995b), pp. 295–297; Neves (1998–1999a), pp. 72–77; Fassò (1970), pp. 113–119.

1.2 The Overcoming of Jus-Naturalism by Jus-Positivism and the Concept of Philosophy of Law

From Ancient Greece to the twentieth-first century legal thinking, determinations of *positive law* by *natural law* have always been present, though stating different material foundations (and contents) and rational meanings. The rational subject/object structure—as proposed by the philosophical constructions since the Ancient Greek, starting from the reference to *sophia* (σοφία)/*phronesis* (φρόνησις) and *episteme* (ἐπιστήμη)/*techne* (τέχνη), and developing in various ways—assumed crucial relevance in the epistemological forms in Modern philosophy, and, specifically within law, in the nineteenth century *Positivisms*.[16]

The perfect assumption of the rational projection of *Natural Law* into the construction of *Positive Law* will be noticed through the ideal of codification: seeing Law as an expression of reason and will, *Natural Law* and Modern rationalism merge in a radical transformation of Law, idealizing it as a rational, complete, codified system.[17] The statutory law should, then, be general, abstract, and formal, as well as clear, and rationally funded and exposed. These characteristics would allow for the statutory law to promote legal security and, therefore, to assume the judge as just the applicant of legal statutes[18]—moving toward the identification of law with legal statutes and of judicial decisions with logical-deductive application.[19]

After the dominant developments of *Juris Naturalis Scientia*, in the pre-Modern and Modern dogmatic structures, a new kind of legal thinking progressively arises, assuming an epistemological rational structure, reaching a prominent position in *Legal Thinking*, as the *Philosophy of Law*. Beyond the reference to *Natural Law* as the result of induction and deduction from an axiom empirically obtained, historically based on substantial presuppositional ethical–moral–theological underpinnings, the rational scope of the *Philosophy of Law* entails a new approach to the foundation of Law, through the proposition of formally rational, nonempirical, and universal groundings.

---

[16] *See* also, on the intellectual virtues in Aristotle, mostly about *sophia* and *phronesis*, Berti (2000), pp. 345–360, and, mostly on the moral virtues and intellectual virtues, on the latter–*techne* (τέχνη), *episteme* (ἐπιστήμη), *phronesis* (φρόνησις), *sophia* (σοφία), and *nous* (νοῦς), Berti (2000), pp. 346–352. « La division de la vertu elle-même se prend de cette division de la partie de l'âme qui a la règle. Nous appelons, en effet, les vertus, les unes vertus de la pensée, les autres vertus du caractere. La philosophie, l'aptitude à comprendre vite, la sagesse, vertus de la pensée; la libéralité et la tempérance, vertus du caractère » - Aristotle (2002), tomo I—*Deuxième Partie: Traduction*; tomo II—*Première Partie, Commentaire: Livres I–IV*; tomo II—*Deuxième Partie, Commentaire: Livres VI–X*. tomo I—*Deuxième Partie: Traduction, cit.*, Livro II–XII, 1103a5, p. 32; Gaudêncio (2019), pp. 58.

[17] Marques (2003), pp. 446 and 528–538.

[18] Marques (1986), pp. 48–49. *See* also Marques (2003), pp. 441–448; Cattaneo (1966), p. 16.

[19] *See* Neves (1995b), pp. 283–335; Marques (2003), pp. 463 ff.; Cattaneo (1966), pp. 13–15.

2 The Foundational Role of *Legal Theory* in the Modern Concept of Law

From the legal and theoretical point of view, the transition to the nineteenth century exposed, both historically and politically, and also technically, the tendency to the assumption of a *positivist scientific method*, determinately influenced by Auguste Comte.[20] Though, the expression *Legal Positivism* denotes, both in the nineteenth century and beyond, a very wide set of concepts of law, in historical and in technical terms, and in linguistic, but also in semiotic and, differently, scientific, legal, and political meanings.[21] The genesis of the *Theory of Law*, as the scientific expression of law developed throughout the nineteenth century, and on, is associated with the emergence of the zetetic character of legal thinking, as Theodor Viehweg has asserted.[22]

In the nineteenth century, the Civil Law system, in the Continental European context, assumed two main positivist expressions, the *École de l'Exégèse* (*School of Exegesis*)—after the French Liberal Revolution, which established the main political and legal underpinnings in Constitutions and the normative specification in codification of the different areas of law—and the *BegriffsJurisprudenz* (*Jurisprudence of Concepts*)—in the German thinking, the nineteenth century, starting from the *Historische Rechtsschule* (*German School of Jurisprudence*), assuming the notion of positive law as a historical consuetudinary acquisition, established on regular practices established through time.[23] Both assume crucial roles in the scientific and academic proposition of *Legal Theory*—in legal construction, in legal interpretation, and in judicial decision.

Generally, *norms* were proposed as *general* and *abstract* normative *criteria* for action, ordered by the authority of the institutionalized instance to enunciate them—in *common law* and in *civil law* systems.[24] The main distinction would, then, be established concerning the norms' origins—whether jurisprudential or legislative.

In Civil Law systems, Law would be understood as *legal norm*, as a general and abstract legal constitutive determination and the criterion for logical-deductive judicial application, while legal thinking would assume a theoretical and logical-apophantic intention, as *legal positivistic science*...[25] Therefore, the law was structured in a logically rational system to which general principles of law and concepts conferred a *horizontal-coherent rational unity*.[26] Norms should be stated as *definitions* of Law, as determinative previsions of *legal reality*. *Legal reality* would then be stated as the *facts* described in *legal norms' texts*, meaning the *defini-*

[20] *See* Comte (1822, 1830–1842, 1844).

[21] *See* Scarpelli (1965), pp. 35, 105, 131.

[22] *See* Viehweg (1968).

[23] Svigny (1814).

[24] *See* Gaudêncio (2020a, b).

[25] Neves (1995b), pp. 307–308.

[26] Neves (1998–1999a), pp. 55–56.

tion of facts in a selection narratively and textually constituted by the text of a norm, as and in the meaning of that textual constitutive substrate—comprehending a literal element as its *substratum*, complemented by the historical, the systematic, and, eventually, the teleological, elements—as Savigny proposed.[27]

Concerning legislative interpretation, legal statutes, assumed as general, abstract, and formal, criteria, with a logical structure—hypothesis and consequence—, therefore as a rational universality structure, should be interpreted in abstract, at a *hermeneutical moment*, logically and temporally before, and independently separated, of the *scientific construction moment* and of the *application moment*. The *scientific moment* would, then, embody the logically constructive stage, using an apophantic method, to propose the induction from norms to obtain general principles and concepts, and the deduction from these latter back to the former ones. These tools of understanding would be concatenated within a logically structured system, which would rationally assume it as the absolute, complete, closed, and logically plain, rational constitution of Law.

The *application moment*, differently, would represent the technical relation established from law, as norm, abstractedly interpreted and logically organized toward general principles and concepts, and reality—understood as fact—, through a syllogistic structure. The rationally constructed legal norm text would, then, be assumed not only as the rational underpinning, but also as the structural criterion of legality, whose creation, assumed by the legislator, and interpretation and systematization, assumed by legal science, would determine the strict and true meaning of law, which the judge should independently, but also formally and deductively, apply.[28]

The French proposal of *École de l'Exégèse* assumed the legal statutes as the key constitutive determinations and criterial orientations to judicial adjudication.[29] In the rationalist natural law, with its intrinsic Modern-Enlightenment concept of law, the *Civil Code* corresponded to the social and political ascension of a social class that was already economically superior. The affirmation of a rational concept of natural law was one of the factors that allowed for the change in the political and legal organization of society. Once this objective was achieved, it was necessary to maintain this situation, to which the *Code Civil* of 1804 contributed greatly, and the affirmation that it was the complete and perfect expression of natural law. All Law would then be enshrined in the *Code*, so that only its text should be considered. The cult of the text was crucial in the *École de l'Exégèse*. The fundamental orientation was an idea of legal purity, linked to an ideal of certainty, which ultimately confines law to legality.[30]

Differently, in the *Begriffsjurisprudenz* proposal, following the *Historische Rechtsschule*, even though the legal statute would also be assumed as a key constitutive determination and criterial orientation to judicial adjudication, it would not

[27] Savigny (1840–1849).

[28] *See* Neves (1995b).

[29] *See* Neves (1995).

[30] *See* Bonnecase (1919) and Gaudêncio (2003).

necessarily be the primordial source of Law. On the other hand, two other tools of understanding would overlap the criterion proposed by the norm, which should be interpreted according to the concept and the system, which would play the role of main tools of understanding, conferring to the law and the legal system a scientific character.[31] As Rudolf von Jhering states, the legal system is a *formal-abstract structure* logically constructed through *legal/(juridical) concepts*, in order to be assumed as an inductive construction of increasingly general and abstract logical formulations.

The aim is to establish of a *Niedere Jurisprudenz*, with juridical propositions and general principles of law, and a *Höhere Jurisprudenz*, with juridical institutes and juridical concepts.[32] And, as Georg Friedrich Puchta designs, the legal system is constituted as a pyramidal structure, also with a logical apophantic *rationale*.[33] In Jhering's quasi-chemical understanding of the juridical system as a formal-abstract structure logically constructed through concepts, the juridical concepts would be inductively obtained from norms, crucially looking for the juridical bodies (*Körper*) as a logical purification of juridical data—both consuetudinary and statutory—, aiming at the construction of *objective law*.[34] These positivist–theoretical–normativistic approaches converged in the general methodological proposal for the rational construction of judicial decision: the *positivist juridical method*.[35]

All of this means that the judicial adjudication would be assumed as a *logical syllogism*, in which the norm, as the major premise—as a rationally universal, general, and abstract logical structure, incorporated into a text, with a hypothesis and a consequence, and operating within a closed, unidimensional, logically complete system of norms—would relate to the fact, as the minor premise, which is the counter-face of the norm. The fact should be acknowledged as an empirical phenomenon, confronted with the hypothesis of the norm as the major premise. If the fact happened to correspond, as a species, to the gender abstractly and generally described by the norm's hypothesis, it would be subsumable, and subsumed, to the norm's hypothesis. To which would, then, the logical conclusion follows: the repetition, in concrete, to the subsumed fact of the legal effect posed by the consequence of the norm in its text.[36]

Within such bases, the decisive contributions of *Allgemeine Rechtslehre*, developed by several authors, proposed legal thinking as a scientifically rational structure, starting from the positivistic scientific method adopted by the empirical–explicative sciences, as a condition for the law and legal thinking to assume the status of science. Therefore, the subject–object rational structure assumed the role of assuring such a status, from an epistemological point of view,

---

[31] Neves (1995a).

[32] *See* Jhering (1852–1865) and Chiassoni (2016).

[33] *See* Puchta (1838); Larenz (1995), pp. 17, 263; Gaudêncio (2022), pp. 98–101.

[34] *See* Jhering (1852–1865); Gaudêncio (2022), pp. 98–101.

[35] *See* Neves (1995b).

[36] *See* Neves (1998–1999a), pp. 59–60; Gaudêncio (2020a, b).

and established the empirical basis for the theoretical construction of universal explicative enunciations of truth as the major aim of legal science. On the other hand, such a scientific character took the legal thinking to an apophantic purpose, of creating scientific principles and concepts starting from the material data law—legal statutes, consuetudinary criteria, jurisprudential criteria. These were the most developed areas of *Legal Science*, in order to assure the apprehension of law into a logically consistent, closed, and self-subsistent legal system.[37]

Adolf Merkel, Ernst Rudolf Bierling, and Karl Bergbohm, in the European Continent,[38] are some of the main authors representing the *General Legal Theory/Theories* construction, the *Allgemeine Rechstlehre(n)/Allgemeine Rechtstheorie*.[39] On the other hand, the *Common Law General Jurisprudence* was developed mainly by John Austin, in the Anglo-American context.[40] And, in the aftermath, new developments were proposed by the Vienna School, mostly in Europe, by Felix Somló, Hans Kelsen, and Georg Jellinek.[41]

The cognitive—subject/ object—rational structure of legal thinking, and the structural systematization of concepts and principles, constitute, at this stage, a crucial part of the scientific construction of *Legal Science*. Adolf Merkel, in his exposition of the *Elements of the Allgemeine Rechstlehre*,[42] emphasizes the concept of objective law—relating the law with the State, explaining the notion of legal thinking, the will and the imperative character of the law, the aims of legal norms, the relation between Law and power; and, after all, the approaching of law as a means to an end: « *Das Recht trägt seinen Zweck nicht in sich selbst* »,[43] which means distinguishing the law as normative order of the purposes to which it can be mobilized, and separating law and power, law and ethics, and establishing the organization of social interests; the positivity of the law and the concept of justice; distinguishing law and State in their nature; the conditions of law and the concept of subjective law(-right).

Specifically, referring law to an end—« *Das Recht ist ein Mittel zum Zweck*(…)»—,[44] Adolf Merkel exposes law as theory (*Lehre*) and a law as power (*Macht*).[45] Under a close approach, Ernst Rudolf Bierling proposes, also within a formalist legal science approach, that the norm is the result of a will—and therefore, proposing a duty, and also that the crucial distinction between objective and subjective law, as well an hierarchical legal structure, which would influence Kelsen.[46] Karl

[37] *See* Neves (1995b).

[38] *See* Funke (2004).

[39] *See* Linhares (2009).

[40] *See* Linhares (2009), p. 268.

[41] Jellinek (1908), Somló (1917) and Kelsen (1960).

[42] *See* Merkel (1899), pp. 577–647.

[43] *See* Merkel (1899), p. 591.

[44] Merkel (1885), p. 13.

[45] *See* Merkel (1885), p. 12.

[46] *See* Bierling (1877–1883, 1894–1917) and Robles-Morchón (2024).

Bergbohm, in turn, also criticizing the *Natural Law Philosophy*, proposes its replacement, beyond the *Historische Rechtsschule*, by a strict juridical thinking[47]: « *Durch die Historische Schule, aber über die Historische Schule hinaus!* ».[48]

In Anglo-American contexts, the Common Law System was intertwined with the Constitution, whether written—as in the United States of America—or non-written—as in the United Kingdom—, and the influences of European codification, as Jeremy Bentham's perspectives show.[49] In a fundamental connection between successive cases and rationes decidendi, within the stare decisis system, even if after this the formalist proposition would require the elaboration of a syllogism to state a deductive application of law. The normativism perspective was then assumed, starting from the consideration of judicial precedents as norms, in their substantially textual construction, and in their characteristically general and abstract logical structure, proposing the codification as the rational ideal construction and exposure of law,[50] and logical deduction as the judicial adjudication rational frame.[51]

Specifically referring to the foundation of law, though, in the Common Law system, John Austin entailed a crucial reflection on the relevance of the distinction between law and morality to the construction of the foundations of Law.[52] A new meaning for *Positivism* and *Non-positivism* was, therefore, being established, assumed through, respectively, the expression of the separation between Law and Morality, and proposing a "command theory," exposing the Law as a legitimate command requiring obedience.[53] And, from a different point of view, Roscoe Pound proposes a more pragmatical perspective on the aims and practices of Law.[54]

The development of positivist legal theories decisively brought the *positivist scientific method* from empirical analytical and explicative sciences to *Legal Thinking*, imposing a new paradigm for legal system and for legal concepts' structure and content. The specific theoretical and methodological cores of such a development of *Legal Theory* were, specifically, the concept of law, the construction of legal norms, of logical concepts and general principles, and of the logical structure of the system.[55]

The zetetic *Theory of Law* developed throughout the nineteenth century constitutes a crucial legacy to the understanding of *Legal Thinking* nowadays. The most relevant development tensions are presented through the evolution from a

---

[47] *See* Bergbohm (1892), pp. 3–25.

[48] Bergbohm (1892), p. 25.

[49] *See* Isaacs (1918), pp. 382–383.

[50] *See* Isaacs (1918), pp. 378–379.

[51] *See* Feldman (2000), p. 83.

[52] Austin (1832, 1885).

[53] Austin (1832), p. 18.

[54] Pound (1912).

[55] *See* (Neves 1998–1999a), pp. 1–27.

subject–object cognitive structure to a subject–subject dialogical structure of philosophical and legal thinking.[56]

3 Beyond *General Theory of Law*: From Positivist Theories of Law to Critical Theories of Law—Macroscopic and Microscopic Perspectives, Procedural and Material Rational Constructions: New Theoretical Perspectives

The meanings and intentions of the theoretical analysis of Law have implied along time very diverse considerations on the fundamental lines of different approaches to the meaning of *Legal Theory*: theoretical orientations (of cognitive–constructivist intentionality, pursued by formalist thoughts), critical–dialectical approaches (of critical–dialectical intentionality)—from the Marxist basis to the neo-Marxist proposals, namely from the *Frankfurt School* and the *Alternative Use of Law* in their original expressions—, among other critical projections within the scope of pluralisms), critical–genealogical views (in the thought of Lyotard, Foucault and Derrida, from the outset, and fundamentally arising from the influence of Nietzsche), and, in a combination of these last two senses of criticism, the *Critical Legal Theories*, mainly, originally, the *Critical Legal Studies Movement*, as a critique of the "liberal" institutionalization of Law and the so-called "Rule of Law."

3.1 Positivism, Non-positivism, and Natural Law

The analysis of the meta-normatively critical–reflexive projections leads to a critical positioning regarding the foundations and normatively theoretical and dogmatic treatments of the dominant themes and intentions in current positive law, as stated, from the confrontation between *Positivisms* and *Non-positivisms*, regarding the relevance of the relations between Morality and Law and some newly arising *Theories of Law*, considering the corresponding historical experiences and political and legal constructions, aiming at a reflection on the fundamental assumptions of the validity and the normativity of law.[57]

Following from the formalist discourses of the *General Theories of Law* that dominated legal thinking in the nineteenth century, the discussion between *Positivism* and *Non-positivism* states itself nowadays by crossing the boundaries among many supposedly specific sense(s) and content(s) of *Moral(s)*, or *Morality(ies)*, on the one hand, and supposedly specific sense(s) and content(s) of

[56] Riedel (1972).

[57] *See* Neves (1998–1999a), pp. 1–31.

law, on the other hand. Such notions of *Morality*, in some cases, and *political morality*, in other cases, are stated as the foundation(s) of Law, the material basis for the construction of legal materials, whether *principles* or *rules*. Therefore, such discussions are present in many conceptions of Law and *Legal Thinking*, from *exclusive positivism* to *inclusive positivism*.[58]

Differently, still in contemporary *Legal Thinking*, assuming *Natural Law* as the foundation of the legal order means posing several questions about the foundational legitimacy and content of law, which receive distinct answers from different statements of natural law, meaning different *Jusnaturalist* theories, hence, *Jusnaturalism(s)*, from the hidden influences of pre-religious (mythological, philosophical, ethical) and later religious matrices, determining a certain culturally shaped context, to the postmodern diverse proposals of natural law theses recovery, from the rationalist to the historical and personalist models.[59]

Natural Law, thought to be a second-order material statement of what the Law is, rather, of what the law is meant to be, is often considered not only as a second nature supra-positive juridical foundation of law, heteronomously introduced as a source of material legitimacy of positive law, but also, in some different way(s), as a second nature supra-positive material nonjuridical foundation of law, rather, effectively, as a moral foundation of law. In both ways, natural law shows itself as some exterior determination of the meaning, the foundation and the content law must present. Therefore, in a non-jusnaturalist meaning of juridicity, even if substantially constructed in the light of a perspective of the axiological foundation of Law and legal *praxis*, from the practical point of view of a (legal) community, the construction of the foundations of law will not be proposed in the same way that, for instance, John Finnis refers to it.[60] Starting from Plato, Aristotle, and Aquinas, Finnis enquires if, even considering law as a social fact, positive law should affirm its foundations to lay on its material content instead of laying on the authority that is allowed to say some regulation to be positive law.[61]

The debate between *Positivism(s)* and *Non-positivism(s)* turns, then, into the relevance of Morality to Law. As Robert Alexy asserts,[62] *Morality* represents a foundational basis of positive law, as law presents a *real or factual dimension*—a dimension of authority and social efficacy—and an *ideal or critical dimension*—understood as *moral correctness*—, stating, from this *dual-nature thesis*, a *non-positivist* approach to law.[63] Such a *dual-nature thesis* remains, though, as an *abstract* reference, needing an integration in a *system* (whose *political structure* would be a *democratic*

[58] Alexy (2010).

[59] *See* Ferrari (2002), mostly pp. 75–93; Bottoni et al. (2017), mainly Chap. 1; Adriani (1988); Borges and Monteiro (2012).

[60] *See* Finnis (2011), p. 23.

[61] Finnis (2011), p. 23.

[62] Alexy (2010).

[63] Alexy (2010), p. 167.

constitutionalism, a *deliberative democracy*) to achieve a *concrete* content and a defined *structure*.[64]

Against the complexity of the definition of these *Positivisms*—based on the presence and/or absence of a *Moral* or *Morality* of commonly diffused outlines—, regardless of whether they are in continuous dialogue or not, the slope of the *liberal rule of law* featured by Ronald Dworkin recognizes Law as an *interpretive concept*.[65] And, so, rejecting the model of autonomization of *Morality* toward *Law*, meaning a *dual systems* perspective (a "*two-systems picture*")—whose statement would be, after all, also compatible with those *Positivisms*, and which was in Dworkin, still underlying, although in differentiation from those, in the enunciation of his *interpretivism*, rather proposing a *single system* perspective ("*one-system picture*"), a "tree-structure," in which Law constitutes a *branch* of *political morality*.[66]

Morality is, then, assumed as a *pervasive concept*—though it is not always clearly stated on its meaning, on its content, nor on the possibilities of its material influence in the determination of meaning and content of juridicity—, taken either as a requirement of the substantial conformation of law or as an instrument for its interpretation and practical realization. In addition, *Morality*, or even *political morality*, are often taken as *Moral*, *tout court*, what might not only cause formal and material irretrievable misunderstandings, but also confer to that *Morality–Moral* an immediate material determinate foundational influence on the material molding and filling of the foundational principles of law, primarily; and, consequently, on juridical criteria, which means to risk a misconstruction and a misinterpretation of the distinction between *Law* and *Moral*, or *Morality*, on the one hand, and an equivocal leveling of communitarian valuations and the relationship they establish with law, on the other hand. And, so, differing from the meanings of the proposal of *inner morality of law*, in the confluence of a *morality of aspiration* and a *morality of duty*, by Lon Fuller, for this latter has its core in the interdependence and reciprocity of the relationship between citizens and the State, and, so, in the reciprocal limits there delineated, therefore conditioning and constituting the *validity of the law*.[67]

The predominantly pressing problems currently addressed by the *Philosophy of Law*, in the Western legal–cultural context, oscillate, then, between three major axes: recoveries of formalist positivism heritage, finalistically ordered substantial instrumentalizations, and axiological references—some based on transcendent inspiration, in various natural law proposals, other of immanent determination, especially of sociological reference, and others of internal legal–material foundation.

---

[64] Alexy (2010), pp. 167–168.

[65] Dworkin (1985); (1986), p. 87; (1996); (2006), pp. 5–21; Neves (2003b), pp. 349–444, especially pp. 349–354. *See* also the more recent developments on the connection between *morality* and *law*, Dworkin (2011), pp. 404–405 (19. «*Law*», 400–415). *See*, also on Dworkin, Postema (2011), pp. 401–456.

[66] Dworkin (2011), pp. 401–402; (1984), pp. 14–45.

[67] *See* Fuller (1969), mostly Ch. 1, pp. 3–32, especially 4–6, 19, 21, and Ch. 2, pp. 33–94, especially 40–42; Postema (2011), pp. 153–162.

The discussion on the necessity, relevance, and/or possibility of objectively determining a foundation for the legal field still leads today—perhaps increasingly so today—to the extreme positions between *Positivist* discourses—although with presuppositions and objectives distinct from those of the nineteenth-century *General Theories of Law*—and *Non-positivist* discourses. This will imply specifying the confrontation between *Positivism(s)* and *Non-positivism(s)*—decisively distinguishing themselves from the formalist discourses of the *General Theories of Law*—in a vast array of densifications of the meaning and content of Law, in more or less openly positivist or more or less openly non-positivist directions.

3.2 *Positivism and Formalism*

Actually, some of the prominent authors of the nineteenth-century *Positivism* were also responsible for the changing of the formalist positivists' perspectives. Rudolf von Jhering played, in such a move, a very important role, while assuming the teleological dimension of Law.[68] Though, several diverse positivist approaches developed throughout the twentieth and the twentieth-first centuries. The discussion on the necessity, relevance, and/or possibility of objectively determining a foundation for the legal field still leads today—perhaps increasingly so today—to the extreme positions between positivist discourses—although with presuppositions and objectives distinct from those of the *General Theories of Law* of the nineteenth century—and non-positivist ones.

The more formalist proposals emphasize the reconstitution of normativist currents—in the continental European matrix, in which the new theories of *Legal Science* stand out, selective heirs of Hans Kelsen's *Pure Theory of Law*,[69] currently with reflections in the proposals of authors such as Matthias Jestaedt[70] and Oliver Lepsius,[71] for instance; and, in the Anglo-American construction, namely the proposals of *Positivism*, *Inclusive*, and *Exclusive*, from the perspective assumed by Wilfrid J. Waluchow,[72] and through the influence of John Austin[73] and Lon Fuller,[74] for example, and branching out into multiple presentations, from

[68] Jhering (1872, 1877) and Seagle (1945).

[69] Kelsen (1960).

[70] *See* Jestaedt (2018), pp. 227–255.

[71] *See* Lepsius (2008).

[72] *See* Waluchow (1994).

[73] *See* Austin (1832).

[74] *See* Fuller (1969).

H.L.A. Hart,[75] on the one hand, to Neil MacCormick,[76] Mathew Kramer,[77] Jules Coleman,[78] and Joseph Raz,[79] among many others—and influencing, for example, Robert Alexy—,[80] and, on the other hand, John Gardner[81] and Leslie Green[82]; making it also necessary to recognize another perspective, of a formalist–normativist bent, proposed, exemplarily, by Frederick Schauer.[83]

Consequently, the analysis of the intersubjective construction and assimilation of the content of validity constituting legality will focus on axiological–normative foundations and political–normative propositions, on the historical connection and (in)evitable (in)separability between these universes—between legal and moral formalism(s) and materialism(s). Seeking, in this second line, a rationally fundamental articulation for the normatively adequate establishment and for the constitution of legality, which can be verified, for example, either in a narratively–normatively interpretative projection of a morally material foundation in a community of principles as objective manifestations of validity assimilated by law as a branch of political morality—as proposed by Ronald Dworkin—,[84] or in a practical-normatively constitutive affirmation of a material foundation autonomously rooted in a community of principles as intersubjective manifestations of validity assimilated by law as a specific normatively practical intentionality—as António Castanheira Neves states.[85]

3.3 *Critical Theories, Neo-formalization and Neo-materialization*

Differently, some of the more materially based proposals, in some cases resulting from direct criticisms of the former, propose a functionalization of Law to externally imposed demands from other regulatory domains of practical life—from politics to economy and/or technology, for instance. Submitting legality to politics, on the one hand—as is the case with the political instrumentalizations of Law, for example, in macroscopically and microscopically structured critical theories: and,

[75] *See* Hart (1994).

[76] *See*, mostly, MacCormick (1997, 2005, 2008).

[77] *See* Kramer (2004).

[78] *See* Coleman (2001a, 2001b, 2007, 2009, 2011).

[79] *See* Raz (2009a, b).

[80] *See*, mostly, Alexy (1983).

[81] *See* Gardner (2012).

[82] *See* Green (1988).

[83] *See*, mostly, Schauer (1991, 2009, 2015).

[84] *See* Dworkin (1986), p. 93; Dworkin (2000), pp. 211–236 (5. «*Liberal Community*»), especially pp. 224–227. See also Neves (2003b), pp. 353, 358, 363–364.

[85] *See*, exemplarily, Neves (2009), pp. 3–28; Neves (2013).

as examples of both, the more moderately assumed, in proposals for a political theory of justice, such as, exemplarily, in John Rawls[86]—as a fundamental element of its *Political Liberalism*—, within the scope of the *overlapping consensus*, and, in the most radically affirmed, such as in the *Critical Legal Studies Movement* and in the multiple *Postmodern Jurisprudences* that followed it, including the *Feminist Jurisprudences and the Critical Race Theories*[87]—mobilizing, as examples, in its founding lines, as regards the first, Roberto Mangabeira Unger, Duncan Kennedy, and Jack Balkin,[88] and, as regards the second, among many others, Robin West, Martha Minow, and Catharine MacKinnon,[89] on the one hand, and Richard Delgado and Jean Stefancic, on the other.[90]

From the point of view of the thematic determination, the discussions concentrate, mainly, in our days, on the one hand, on analyzing the counterpoint between *liberalisms* and *communitarianisms*, and, on the other hand, and consequently, on late-modern proposals of generalized individualization—*neo-liberalisms*, *libertarianisms*, and *populisms*—and *postmodern alternatives* of microscopically stylized subjectivization, which leads to the analysis of the confrontations between the considered majority, or hegemonic, or dominant, or central, options, in the face of minority, or marginal, or peripheral, proposals—such as, exemplarily, some developments in critical theories, namely feminist theories, critical race theories, and theories of decolonization. Or, on the other hand, though still linked with the contemporary complexity of intersubjective encountering, however from a more individualist point of view, submitting legality to economy—as in the *Economic Analysis of Law*, with Ronald Coase,[91] Richard Posner,[92] Guido Calabresi,[93] among others, stands out exponentially. Or even to technology—in the finalist perspective that, for example, Hans Albert proposes,[94] under the influence of epistemology and Karl Popper's proposition of an open society.[95] And even to ethics—the ethics of duties, of otherness, of care (with Martha Nussbaum,[96] Amalia Amaya,[97] Nancy Fraser,[98] or Axel Honneth,[99] among others). Among many other practical

[86] *See* Rawls (2005).

[87] More developments in Gaudêncio (2013).

[88] *See*, initially Unger (1983), Kennedy (1998), Balkin (1986, 1987); Altman (1990) and Pérez Lledó (1996).

[89] *See*, among many others, Bartlett and Kennedy (1991).

[90] *See*, exemplarily Delgado and Stefancic (2017).

[91] Coase (1960, 1994).

[92] Posner (1990, 1995, 2001, 2003).

[93] Calabresi (1970).

[94] Albert (1968, 1978).

[95] Popper (1971).

[96] Mostly Nussbaum (2006, 2011).

[97] Amaya and Lay (2012) and Amaya and Mar (2020).

[98] Fraser (2009) and Fraser and Honneth (2003).

[99] Honneth (2003, 2000, 2010, 2015).

determinations currently under development are aesthetic perspectives of intersubjectivity (illustrated, for example, in the recent evolution of Peter Goodrich's thought).[100]

In the current contexts of plurality—even of pluralisms, and relativisms—, practice has also been manifesting some other tendencies to reduce the relevance of material valuation, compromising the possibility of substantially positive intervention of the legal discipline, progressively relegated to a proceduralization, as a formal framework, oscillating between waves of neo-materialization of law, with the various material legal functionalisms—to say it with António Castanheira Neves, inserting Law as an instrument and/or as a regulatory discourse among other equally possible ones, directed toward externally imposed ends… —, and waves of neo-formalization, as a reaction to that neo-materialization, with formal legal functionalisms—such as that proposed by Niklas Luhmann.[101]

Though not necessarily assuming an autonomous rational structure and substantial foundation to Law and *Legal Theory*, some other proposals affirm distinct orders of values, as axiological foundations, referencing materially founding orders, positively and negatively delimiting, whether of a transcendent nature—theistic or cosmological, tending toward ontological and deontological—, or of sociological reference—with an empirical–immanent intent—, or of a legal-materially internal foundation. What today extends from neo-Thomist perspectives—as, for example, in Michel Villey,[102] on the one hand, and in John Finnis,[103] although very differently, on the other—to neo-Kantian ones—with Gustav Radbruch[104] and Arthur Kaufmann,[105] for example—, and with fundamental projections in understandings based on ethical personalism, both with and without theological bases.[106]

From the dialogue within such proposals, and considering their possibilities and contributions, some alternative directions seek to follow an internal legal–material foundation in *Legal Theory*, such as the one posed by Ronald Dworkin,[107] and the one stated by António Castanheira Neves. Following this latter, searching for a normatively and materially autonomous foundation to Law and *Legal Theory*, implies starting from the diagnosis of the *crisis of the Philosophy of Law within the context of the global crisis of Philosophy*,[108] and establishing fundamental dialogues with *Normativisms*, *Functionalisms*, and *Jurisprudentialisms*,[109] based on the norma-

[100] Goodrich (1987, 2017); Douzinas et al. (1994); Neves (1995c).

[101] Luhmann (1984, 1986, 1989, 1993); Neves (1998–1999a), pp. 70–106.

[102] Villey (1962, 1975).

[103] *See* Finnis (2011).

[104] Radbruch (1932).

[105] Kaufmann (1997).

[106] Bowne (1908); Buford and Oliver (2002); McLean (1996); Mounier (2011).

[107] *See*, finally, Dworkin (2011).

[108] *See* Neves (2003a).

[109] *See* Neves (1998–1999a, 1998–1999b); Neves (2013); Linhares (2012a, 2012b, 2016), pp. 227–249.

tively material underpinnings of Law, and on its specific type of rationality and *modus operandi*, reflecting the theoretical structuring and the practical positioning of Law and *Legal Thinking* on an autonomous normatively constitutive intention, between a reflexive–speculative perspective, from the *Philosophy of Law*, and a critical–reflexive perspective, from the *Theory of Law*.[110]

4 Conclusions: Legal Theory Legal Autonomy

This approach intended to address the origins of the *General Theory of Law* as a field of reflection dedicated to understanding the role of Law and its relationship with *Legal Science*. The chapter asserts that the notion of a *General Theory of Law* arose mostly as a result of modern history, with the purpose of granting *reflective autonomy* to Law, and that, therefore, throughout the nineteenth century, it would express itself through *methodological structures* that disconnected Law from reality dimensions. This movement was an important step in the construction of the identity of *Legal Science*, as well as in the determination of an unequivocal disconnection from the legacy of *Natural Law*, especially since modern codification.

The various *Positivist* theoretical approaches, until and still nowadays, continue this demand for *methodology* and *autonomy*. Contrary to the belief that theoretical currents have stalled at this point in the discussion, a plethora of contemporary trends is considered, within the countless *schools of thought* dedicated to debating the role of *Legal Theory*: *Positivism, Non-positivism, Natural Law, Formalism, Law and Economics, Feminism, Critical Theory, Postmodern*, among others.

Such map and global critique aimed to highlight the vast complexity of the issue, which remains open as a provocative dimension surrounding the debate on the nature, the foundations and the autonomy of Law and Legal Theory in our times.

References

Adriani M (1988) Storia delle religioni. Nardini Editore, Firenze

Albert H (1968–1991) Traktat über kritische Vernunft. Mohr Siebeck, Tübingen

Albert H (1978) Traktat über rationale praxis. Mohr Siebeck, Tübingen

Alexy R (1983) Theorie der juristischen argumentation. Die Theorie des rationalen Diskurs als Theorie der juristischen Begründung. Suhrkamp, Frankfurt am Main

Alexy R (2010) The dual nature of law. Ratio Juris 23(2):167–182

Altman A (1990) Critical legal studies. A liberal critique. Princeton University Press, Princeton

Amaya A, Lay HH (eds) (2012) Law, virtue and justice. Hart Publishing, Bloomsbury

Amaya A, Mar M (eds) (2020) Virtue, emotion and imagination in law and legal reasoning. Hart Publishing, Bloomsbury

[110] *See* Neves (1998–1999a), pp. 1–31.

Aristotle (2002) L'Éthique à Nicomaque, 2nd edn. Traduction René Antoine Gauthier, Jean Yves Jolif. Peeters, Nauwelaert. Louvain-la Neuve
Austin J (1832) The province of jurisprudence determined. John Murray, London
Austin J (1885) Lectures on jurisprudence or the philosophy of positive law, 5th edn. John Murray, London
Balkin J (1986) The crystalline structure of legal thought. Rutgers Law Rev 39(1):1–103
Balkin J (1987) Deconstructive practice and legal theory. Yale Law J 96(4):743–786
Bartlett KT, Kennedy R (eds) (1991) Feminist legal theory. Readings in law and gender. Routledge, New York
Bergbohm C (1892) Jurisprudenz und Rechtsphilosophie. Kritische Abhandlungen. Dunker und Humblot, Leipzig
Berti E (2000) The reception of Aristotle's intellectual virtues. Rev Port Filos 56:345–360
Bierling E (1877–1883) Zur Kritik der juristischen Grundbegriffe, 2 Bände. Perthes, Gotha
Bierling E (1894–1917) Juristische Prinzipienlehre, 5 Bände. Freiburg i. B., Leipzig. Mohr, Tübingen
Bonnecase J (1919) L'École de l'Exégèse en Droit Civil. E. de Boccard Éditeur, Paris
Borges A, Monteiro JG (2012) As três religiões do livro. Imprensa da Universidade de Coimbra, Coimbra
Bottoni R, Cristofori R, Ferrari S (eds) (2017) Religious rules, state law, and normative pluralism: a comparative view. Springer, Cham
Bowne BP (1908) Personalism. Houghton Mifflin Company, Boston
Buford TO, Oliver HH (eds) (2002) Personalism revisited: its proponents and critics. Editions Rodopi, Amsterdam
Calabresi G (1970) The cost of accidents. A legal and economic analysis. Yale University Press, Yale
Cattaneo MA (1966) Illuminismo e legislazione. Edizioni di Communità, Milano
Chiassoni P (2016) Rudolf von Jhering. In: Pattaro E, Roversi C (eds) Legal philosophy in the twentieth century: the civil law world. Vol 12. Tome 2, pp 590–597
Coase R (1960) The problem of social cost. J Law Econ 03:1–44
Coase R (1994) Essays on economics and economists. The University of Chicago Press, Chicago
Coleman J (ed) (2001a) Hart's postscript. Essays on the postscript to the concept of law. Oxford University Press, Oxford
Coleman J (2001b) The practice of principle. In: Defence of a pragmatist approach to legal theory. Oxford University Press, Oxford
Coleman J (2007) Beyond the separability thesis: moral semantics and the methodology of jurisprudence. Oxf J Leg Stud 27:581–608
Coleman J (2009) Beyond inclusive legal positivism. Ratio Juris 22(3):359–394
Coleman J (2011) The architecture of jurisprudence. Yale Law J 121(1):1–80
Comte A (1822) Plan des travaux scientifiques nécessaires pour réorganiser la société. In: de Saint-Simon H (ed) Suite des travaux ayant pour objet de fonder le système industriel. Du Contrat social. Les marchands de nouveautés, Paris
Comte A (1830–1842) Cours de philosophie positive. Bachelier, Paris
Comte A (1844) Discours sur l'esprit positif. Carilian-Gœury et V. Dalmont, Paris
Delgado R, Stefancic J (2017) Critical race theory. An introduction, 3rd edn. New York University Press, New York
Douzinas C, Goodrich P, Hachamovitch Y (1994) Politics, postmodernity and critical legal studies: the legality of the contingent. Routledge, London
Dworkin R (1984) Taking rights seriously. Harvard University Press, Cambridge
Dworkin R (1985) A matter of principle. Harvard University Press, Cambridge
Dworkin R (1986) Law's empire. Harvard University Press, Cambridge
Dworkin R (1996) Objectivity and truth: you'd better believe it. Philos Public Aff 25(2):87–139
Dworkin R (2000) Sovereign virtue. The theory and practice of equality. Harvard University Press, Cambridge
Dworkin R (2006) Justice in robes. Harvard University Press, Cambridge

Dworkin R (2011) Justice for hedgehogs. Harvard University Press, Cambridge
Fassò G (1970) Storia della Filosofia del Diritto—Volume III: Ottocento e Novecento. Il Mulino, Bologna
Feldman S (2000) American legal thought from premodernism to postmodernism. An intellectual voyage. Oxford University Press, Oxford
Ferrari S (2002) Lo spirito dei diritti religiosi. Il Mulino, Bologna
Finnis J (2011) Natural law and natural rights. Oxford University Press, Oxford
Fraser N (2009) Scales of justice: reimagining political space in a globalizing world. Columbia University Press, New York
Fraser N, Honneth A (2003) Umverteilung oder Anerkennung? Eine politisch-philosophische kontroverse. Suhrkamp, Frankfurt am Main
Fuller L (1969) The morality of law. Yale University Press, New Haven
Funke A (2004) Allgemeine Rechtslehre als juristische Strukturtheorie: Entwicklung und gegenwärtige Bedeutung der Rechtstheorie um 1900. Mohr Siebeck, Tübingen
Gardner J (2012) Law as a leap of faith: essays on law in general. Oxford University Press, Oxford
Gaudêncio AM (2003) O culto do texto da lei na Escola da Exegese: seu sentido e limites. Boletim da Faculdade de Direito da Universidade de Coimbra 79:681–733
Gaudêncio AM (2013) Entre o centro e a periferia: a perspectivação ideológico-política da dogmática jurídica e da decisão judicial no Critical Legal Studies Movement. Lumen Juris, Rio de Janeiro
Gaudêncio AM (2019) O intervalo da tolerância nas fronteiras da juridicidade: fundamentos e condições de possibilidade da projecção jurídica de uma (re)construção normativamente substancial da exigência de tolerância. Instituto Jurídico da Faculdade de Direito da Universidade de Coimbra, Coimbra
Gaudêncio AM (2020a) Jurisdictional realization of law as Judicium: a methodological alternative, beyond deductive application and finalistic decision. Int J Semiot Law 33(1):133–146
Gaudêncio AM (2020b) From the norms-fact dichotomy to the system-problem connection in the judicial realisation of law: logical deduction v. analogical judgment in adjudication. In: Condello A (ed) New rhetorics for contemporary legal discourse. Edinburgh University Press, Edinburgh, pp 37–49
Gaudêncio AM (2022) Presumption(s) of correctness(?): comparing the methodological relevance of precedents in civil law and in common law systems. In: Bersier N, Bezemek C, Schauer F (eds) Common law—civil law: the great divide? Springer, Cham, pp 95–116
Gilissen J (1979) Introduction historique au Droit. Établissements Émille Bruyant, Bruxelles
Goodrich P (1987) Legal discourse: studies in linguistics. Rhetoric and legal analysis. The Macmillan Press (1990), London
Goodrich P (2017) Imago decidendi: on the common law of images. Brill, Leiden
Green L (1988) The authority of the state. Clarendon Press, Oxford
Grotius H (1625) De jure belli ac pacis libri tres, in quibus jus naturae et gentium, item juris publici praecipua explicantur. Paris
Hart HLA (1994) The concept of law, 2nd edn. Oxford University Press, Oxford
Honneth A (2000) Das Andere der Gerechtigkeit. Aufsätze zur praktischen Philosophie. Suhrkamp, Frankfurt am Main
Honneth A (2003) Kampf um Anerkennung. Zur moralischen Grammatik sozialer Konflikte, 2.ed edn. Suhrkamp, Frankfurt am Main
Honneth A (2010) Das Ich im Wir. Studien zur Anerkennungstheorie. Suhrkamp, Frankfurt am Main
Honneth A (2015) Die Idee des Sozialismus. Suhrkamp, Berlin
Isaacs N (1918) The schools of jurisprudence: their places in history and their present alignment. The quarrels of the "schools". Harv Law Rev 31(3):373–411
Jellinek G (1908) Die sozialethische Bedeutung von Recht, Unrecht und Strafe, 2nd edn. O. Häring, Berlin

Jestaedt M (2018) Vom Beruf der Rechtswissenschaft—zwischen Rechtspraxis und Rechtstheorie. In: Dreier H (ed) Rechtswissenschaft als Beruf. Mohr Siebeck, Tübingen, pp 227–255

Jhering R (1852–1865) Geist des römischen Rechts auf den verschiedenen Stufen seiner Entwicklung, 4.ed edn. Breitkopf & Härtel, Leipzig

Jhering R (1872) Der Kampf ums Recht. Vittorio Klostermann, Frankfurt am Main

Jhering R (1877) Der Zweck im Recht. Erster Band. Breitkopf & Härtel, Leipzig

Kant I (1788) Kritik der praktischen Vernunft. Johann Friedrich Hartknoch, Riga

Kant I (1797–1798) Die Metaphysik der Sitte. Friedrich Nicolovius, Königsberg

Kaufmann A (1997) Rechtsphilosophie. C. H. Beck, München

Kelsen H (1960) Reine Rechtslehre: Einleitung in die rechtswissenschaftliche Problematik. Deutick, Leipzig, Wien

Kennedy D (1998) A critique of adjudication. Harvard University Press, Harvard

Kramer MH (2004) Where law and morality meet. Oxford University Press, Oxford

Larenz K (1995) Methodenlehre der Rechtswissenschaft, 3rd edn. Springer, Berlin

Lepsius O (2008) Themen einer Rechtswissenschaftstheorie. In: Jestaedt M, Lepsius O (eds) Rechtswissenschaftstheorie. Mohr Siebeck, Tübingen, pp 1–50

Linhares JMA (2009) Os desafios-feridas da Allgemeine Rechtslehre. Um tempo de teoria do direito reconhecido (reencontrado?) pela perspectiva de outro tempo de teoria. In: Alves JL et al (eds) Liber Amicorum de José de Sousa e Brito em comemoração do 70° aniversário. Coimbra, Almedina, pp 61–314

Linhares JMA (2012a) Law's cultural project and the claim to universality or the equivocalities of a familiar debate. Int J Semiot Law 25:489–503

Linhares JMA (2012b) Na 'coroa de fumo' da teoria dos princípios: poderá um tratamento dos princípios como normas servir-nos de guia? In: Alves JL et al (eds) Estudos em Homenagem ao Professor Doutor José Joaquim Gomes Canotilho, Stvdia Ivridica, vol III. Coimbra Editora, Coimbra, pp 395–421

Linhares JMA (2016) 'Juízo ou decisão?': uma interrogação condutora no(s) mapa(s) do discurso jurídico contemporâneo. In: Bronze FJ et al (eds) Juízo ou decisão? O problema da realização jurisdicional do direito. Instituto Jurídico da Faculdade de Direito da Universidade de Coimbra, Coimbra, pp 227–249

Luban D (1997) Legal modernism. University of Michigan Press, Michigan

Luhmann N (1984) Soziale systeme. Grundriß einer allgemeinen Theorie. Suhrkamp, Frankfurt am Main

Luhmann N (1986) L'unité du système juridique. Archives de Philosophie du Droit 31:163–188

Luhmann N (1989) Le Droit comme système social. Droit et Société 11–12:53–66

Luhmann N (1993) Das Recht der Gesellschaft. Suhrkamp, Frankfurt am Main

MacCormick N (1997) Legal reasoning and legal theory. Oxford University Press, Oxford

MacCormick N (2005) Rhetoric and the rule of law. A theory of legal reasoning. Oxford University Press, Oxford

MacCormick N (2008) Practical reason in law and morality. Oxford University Press, Oxford

Marques MR (1986) O Liberalismo e a codificação do direito civil em Portugal. Boletim da Faculdade de Direito da Universidade de Coimbra, Coimbra 29:1–256

Marques MR (2003) Codificação e paradigmas da modernidade. Coimbra Editora, Coimbra

McLean GF (ed) (1996) Personalist ethics and human subjectivity. Council for Research in Values and Philosophy, Washington

Merkel (1885) Juristische encyclopädie. J. Guttentag, Berlin

Merkel A (1899) Gesammelte Abhandlungen aus dem Gebiet der allgemeinen Rechtslehre und des Strafrechts. Verlag von Karl J. Trübner, Strassburg

Mounier E (2011) Personalism. Read Books Ltd, Warwickshire

Neves AC (1995) A Escola da Exegese. Dig 2:181–191

Neves AC (1995a) A Escola Histórica do Direito. Dig 2:203–214

Neves AC (1995b) Método Jurídico. Dig 2:283–336

Neves AC (1995c) A redução política do pensamento metodológico-jurídico (Breves notas críticas sobre o seu sentido). Dig 2:379–421

Neves A C (1998–1999a) Teoria do direito. Coimbra Editora, Coimbra
Neves A C (1998–1999b) Apontamentos complementares de Teoria do Direito. Coimbra Editora, Coimbra
Neves AC (2003a) A crise actual da Filosofia do Direito no contexto da crise global da Filosofia. Tópicos para a possibilidade de uma reflexiva reabilitação, Stvdia Ivridica, 72. Coimbra Editora, Coimbra
Neves AC (2003b) Dworkin e a interpretação jurídica—ou a interpretação jurídica, a hermenêutica e a narratividade. In: Neves AC (ed) O actual problema metodológico da interpretação jurídica. Coimbra Editora, Coimbra
Neves AC (2009) Pensar o direito num tempo de perplexidade. In: Dias AS et al (eds) Liber Amicorum de José de Sousa e Brito, em comemoração do 70. Aniversário, Almedina, Coimbra, pp 3–28
Neves AC (2013) O direito como validade: a validade como categoria jurisprudencialista. Revista da Faculdade de Direito da Universidade Federal do Ceará 34(2):39–76
Nussbaum M (2006) Frontiers of justice: disability, nationality, species membership. Harvard University Press, Harvard
Nussbaum M (2011) Creating capabilities. The human development approach. Harvard University Press, Harvard
Pérez Lledó JA (1996) El movimiento Critical Legal Studies. Tecnos, Madrid
Popper K (1971) The open society and its enemies. Princeton University Press, Princeton
Posner R (1990) The problems of jurisprudence. Harvard University Press, Harvard
Posner R (1995) Overcoming law. Harvard University Press, Harvard
Posner R (2001) The problematics of moral and legal theory. Harvard University Press, Harvard
Posner R (2003) Law, pragmatism and democracy. Harvard University Press, Harvard
Postema GJ (2011) Legal philosophy in the twentieth century: the common law world. In: Pattaro E (ed) A treatise of legal philosophy and general jurisprudence, 11. Springer, New York
Pound R (1912) Theories of law. Yale Law J 22(2):114–150
Puchta G (1838) Lehrbuch der Pandekten. Johann Ambrosius Barth, Leipzig
Pufendorf S (1672) De iure naturae et gentium libri octo. London
Radbruch G (1932) Rechtsphilosophie. Von Quelle & Meyer, Leipzig
Rawls J (2005) Political liberalism. 2nd edn. Columbia University Press, New York
Raz J (2009a) Between authority and interpretation. On the theory of law and practical reason. Oxford University Press, Oxford
Raz J (2009b) The authority of law. Essays on law and morality, 2.ed edn. Oxford University Press, Oxford
Riedel M (1972) Rehabilitierung der praktischen Philosophie. Rombach, Freiburg im Breisgau
Robles-Morchón G (2024) La influencia de la obra de Ernst R. Bierling en la Escuela Jurídica de Viena. Ars Interpretandi: Rivista di ermeneutica giuridica 1:65–74
Rousseau J (1762) Du contrat social ou principes du droit politique. Marc-Michel Rey, Amsterdam
Savigny FK (1840–1849) System des heutigen römischen Rechts. Veit, Berlin
Scarpelli U (1965) Cos'è il positivismo giuridico. Edizioni di Comunità, Milano
Schauer F (1991) Playing by the rules. A philosophical examination of rule-based decision making in law and in life. Clarendon Press, Oxford
Schauer F (2009) Thinking like a lawyer. A new introduction to legal reasoning. Harvard University Press, Harvard
Schauer F (2015) The force of law. Harvard University Press, Harvard
Schultz F (1953) History of roman legal science. Clarendon Press, Oxford
Seagle W (1945) Rudolf von Jhering: or law as a means to an end. University of Chicago Law Review 13(1)
Truyol y Serra (1954) Súmula da história da filosofia do direito. Revista da Faculdade de Direito da Universidade de Lisboa 10:58–81
Somló F (1917) Juristische Grundlehre. Felix Meiner, Leipzig
Svigny FK (1814) Vom Beruf unserer Zeit für Gesetzgebung und Rechtswissenschaft. Mohr und Zimmer, Heidelberg

Thomasius C (1705) Fundamenta Juris Naturae et Gentium ex Sensu Communi Deducta, in quibus ubique secernuntur principia honesti, justi ac decori, cum adjuncta emendatione ad ista fundamenta institutionum jurisprudentia divinae. Halae

Unger RM (1983) The critical legal studies movement. Harv Law Rev 96(3):563–675

Viehweg T (1968) Systemprobleme in Rechtsdogmatik und Rechtsforschung. Studien Wissenschaftstheorie, 2. Meisenheim am Glan, Hain

Villey M (1962) Leçons d'histoire de la philosophie du droit, 2nd edn. Dalloz, Paris

Villey M (1975) La formation de la pensée juridique moderne. Montchrétien, Paris

Waluchow W (1994) Inclusive legal positivism. Oxford University Press, Oxford

Wieacker F (1952) Privatrechtsgeschichte der Neuzeit unter besonderer Berücksichtigung der deutschen Entwicklung. Vandenhoeck u. Ruprecht, Göttingen

Wolff C (1750) Institutiones Juris Naturae et Gentium, in quibus ex ipsa hominis natura continuo nexu omnes obligationes et Jura omnia deducuntur. Halle

Ana Margarida Simões Gaudêncio Associate Professor, *Faculty of Law*, *University of Coimbra* (Portugal). Degree in Law, from the *Faculty of Law* of the *University of Coimbra* (1999). Master's Degree in Law, in the area of Legal and Philosophical Sciences, from the *Faculty of Law* of the *University of Coimbra* (2005). PhD in Law, in the speciality of Legal–Philosophical Sciences, from the *Faculty of Law* of the *University of Coimbra* (2014).

The Metascientific Discourse of the *General Theory of Law*: The Relationship Between General Theory and Special Theories

Eduardo C. B. Bittar

Abstract This chapter analyzes the General Theory of Law from a discursive approach, emphasizing the importance of the reciprocal contribution between the Semiotics of Law and the General Theory of Law. The metascientific legal language is analyzed as a component of the discourse of the General Theory of Law. In this interpellation, the text dialogues intensely with the contributions of Algirdas Julien Greimas, Peter Goodrich, Dominique Maingueneau, Maria Giulia Dondero and Jerzy Wroblewski. Throughout its analysis, the chapter is dedicated to understanding the relationship between the General Theory and the Special Theories, which have emerged in contemporary context, and which, gradually, are taking over the place of the General Theories of Specialities of the Science of Law. This point is placed at the center of the analysis, insofar as what is observed is that the scientific universe in the field of Law is expanding, which has implied an increase in the branching of new fields of the Science of Law. In this context of transformations, it is debated whether the General Theory of Law is outdated and has lost its discursive place, in the face of the multiplication of the General Theories of Specialities. In fact, there is a repositioning, which needs to be analyzed and exposed, of the General Theory of Law as a federative science of specialized legal knowledge. With this, the reflexive force and the resolutive force begin to coordinate more harmoniously, in the process of adapting the General Theory of Law to current challenges. This Chapter is also dedicated to understanding the specific discursive nature of the scientific enunciation of the General Theory of Law, descending toward an exhaustive study of its specific qualities, which are: i.) universal statements; ii.) abstract statements; iii.) empirical-analytical statements; iv.) theoretical statements; v.) rational and demonstrative statements; vi.) complex statements; vii.) unifying statements; viii.) general statements; ix.) polemic statements; and x.) argumentative statements. In the context of the rise of algorithmic rationality, the process of dehumanization

Chapter translated by Kavita Lamba.

E. C. B. Bittar (✉)
Faculty of Law, University of São Paulo, São Paulo, São Paulo, Brazil

E. C. B. Bittar (ed.), *General Theory of Law*,
https://doi.org/10.1007/978-3-032-22517-7_2

of the Science of Law is discussed and the figure of the jurist-Prometheus is also discussed. Finally, this chapter also discusses the role of a Theory of Humanistic Realism within the framework of General Theory of Law, and its critical task of preparing legal professionals for humanization and the exercise of reflective power, at a time when the rationality inherent in the Science of Law is being eroded.

1 Introduction: Science, Method, and Discourse

The notion of a legal system has changed, the modalities of legal sources are being rediscussed, rules and principles have been integrated into the logic of the legal system, the techniques for resolving antinomies are being revised, and judicial precedents have earned a prominent place in the judicial universe. To summarize briefly, it can be seen that the understanding of law is changing, while the understanding of the role of the *General Theory of Law* has remained relatively constant. In this respect, the effort to *reconstruct* the *General Theory of Law*, in times of *crisis of meaning*, deserves to be carried out as a form of *resignification*. The task of *resignification* also includes a task of *renewal*. This, in turn, implies an attitude of *repositioning* in time and history, *revisiting* traditional concepts and analyzing new perspectives. Hence, for the purpose of *resignification*, the task of reflection on the *current status* of the *General Theory of Law* is included, aimed at resynchronizing its *discursive function* in relation to other *legal discourses*. Here is an assessment that the *General Theory of Law* is an advanced form of legal knowledge, indispensable to the self-understanding that jurists must have of their universe of work, being responsible for a field of work, which is not covered by any other area of legal knowledge.

As an initial starting point, it should be borne in mind that the *discursive place* of the *General Theory of Law* has been established, among jurists, in that, since its creation, this field has not been occupied by any other discipline from which a relevant epistemological claim to the contrary has arisen. Despite the stability and continuity of its *discursive place*, it is true that there are variations, when it comes to adopting the *signifier* to identify the area (*General Jurisprudence*; *Legal Theory*; *Theory of Law*; *Allgemeine Rechtslehre*; *Théorie Générale du Droit*; *Teoria Generale del Diritto*; *Teoría General del Derecho*). Moreover, it has to be said, the divergences do not stop at the level of the *signifier*, a huge group of other questions are also causing controversy, such as the question of the scope of the discipline, the method of the discipline, the function of the discipline, and the relationship of the discipline with other areas of Law.[1]

In this study, the aim is to revisit the subject, adopting the point of view that Law is a *discursive system*, a *system of legal texts* interconnected among themselves,

[1] "'Jurisprudence', 'legal theory', and 'legal philosophy' do not have settled meanings in either the Anglo-American or the Continental European traditions" (Twining 2005, p. 656).

which carry out discursive operations such as a *discursive machine*.[2] Law is a discourse in practice and, also, in theory. This way, research into Law implies analyzing a high degree of reciprocal entanglement among the various forms of *legal discourse*. In particular, the analysis undertaken here will seek to emphasize the understanding of the *General Theory of Law* as a *theoretical–philosophical discourse* regarding *legal discourse*. In these terms, this approach presupposes a scientific contribution external to the *General Theory of Law* and is able to investigate the status of *theoretical–philosophical discourse*. This is how the task can be performed by approaching the relationship of *Law & Language*, implying the approximation between the *Semiotics of Law* research and the *General Theory of Law* research—following the clue left by Peter Goodrich[3] and Bernard Jackson[4]—, in an encounter that has proved fertile for dealing with the nature of *legal discourses*.

The interconnection between these fields is well defined, assuming that, for *Semiotics*, *Law* can be considered a field of application by its concepts and categories.[5] As a result, what can be seen is that the *General Theory of Law* can only gain from this interdisciplinary cooperation, insofar as it has been understood, in connection with the *Semiotics of Law*, as a theory that analyzes the process of the self-construction of *legal discourse*, following the line of analysis by Pierre Moor.[6] Despite recognizing the existence of horizons of distancing and approximation, the *General Theory of Law* has been nourished by original contributions brought by the *Semiotics of Law*, as previous studies have shown.[7]

In the Greimasian line of approach, *Semiotics* takes on the role of a *discursive epistemology*,[8] having *legal discourse* as a field of work. This is how this chapter will be dedicated to analyzing the subject chosen as an object of research, which is: *The metascientific discourse of the General Theory of Law*. The subtitle indicates a specific problem, namely, the discussion about the relationship between *General Theory* and *Special Theories*, considering the increasing complexity of the universe of meaning in Law. In order to tackle this problem, throughout the development of the chapter, the analysis will have to be unfolded, bearing in mind the arguments contained in the following topics: in item 2 (*The current situation and the crisis of*

[2] Cf. Bittar (2024a, b), pp. 159–178.

[3] See Goodrich (1984a, b), pp. 173–206.

[4] *Vide* Jackson (1985).

[5] "One could conclude at first glance, that law is an important *area of application* for semiotics insight in signs and symbols" (Broekman and Backer 2013, p. 08).

[6] "Nous dirons: la théorie du droit comme théorie du travail de la production du droit" (Moor 2010, p. 304).

[7] Cf. Bittar (2023), pp. 04–05.

[8] "L'épistémologie discursive, que je m'efforce de définir et de démontrer depuis quelques années, se distingue des deux autres, car elle reprend le point de vue immanent au langage. Ma compréhension actuelle de cette épistémologie me conduit à penser qu'elle investiguerait, dans les structures, de discours en discours, les astuces de l'énonciation, c'est-à-dire la (les) rationalité(s) discursive(s) opérant dans tout acte de langage, dans tout acte d'expérience (même scientifique), dans tout acte de réflexion cogitante, bref, dans tout acte humain de perception du monde et du corps" (Beividas 2019, p. 93).

meaning of the General Theory of Law), it will seek to analyze and discuss the question of the crisis of meaning of the *General Theory of Law*, assessing the extent to which the lack of relevance threatens the *discursive place* of the area; in item 3 (*The discursive relationship between the General Theory of Law and the General Theories of Specialities*), it will seek to understand how the *Science of Law* advances and progresses, explaining the phenomenon of the emergence and dissemination of the *General Theories of Specialities*, which demands a new approach to the position of the *General Theory of Law* in relation to them; in item 4 (*The discursive polyglotism and the all-encompassing of the General Theory of Law*), the analysis will focus on the function of the *General Theory of Law* in relation to other legal dogmatics, seeking to discuss the range of the area's perspective; in item 5 (*Theoretical discourse and the metalanguage of the General Theory of Law*), it will seek to investigate the *theoretical discourse* that is specific to the *General Theory of Law*, considering its metascientific nature; in item 6 (*The figure of the jurist-Prometheus and algorithmic rationality*), the investigation will be directed toward understanding the challenges of the digital era and posthumanism, conceiving the ideal figure of the *jurist-Prometheus*, from which the exercise of *algorithmic rationality* in the field of the *Science of Law* is discussed; in item 7 (*Algorithmic rationality and the reflexive force of the General Theory of Law*), it proceeds toward criticizing technoscience, thereby recovering the reflexive force of the *General Theory of Law*; in item 8 (*The humanization of the General Theory of Law: an understanding from the Theory of Realistic Humanism*), from the perspective of the *Theory of Realistic Humanism*, it seeks to take a stand and develop the conditions of the process of *humanizing* legal reasoning, in times of technoscience, in order to reaffirm the importance of thought, *prudential reasoning* and the *place of discourse* of the *General Theory of Law*, in the midst of scientific discourses of the *Science of Law*.

2 The Current Situation and the Crisis of Meaning of the *General Theory of Law*

2.1 The General Theory of Law: Crisis, Anachronism, Lack of Relevance

Since its emergence, the *General Theory of Law* has gone through the most diverse phases. It can be understood that, as a necessary tool for jurists, its phases of internal development can be divided as follows: (1) discovery phase, (2) consolidation phase, (3) vulgarization phase. In the first phase (nineteenth century), this field of theoretical work was marked by great innovation, disassociating itself from the *Philosophy of Law*,[9] whereas in the second phase (twentieth century), it was marked by qualifying the method and amplification of the audience, and, finally, in the third

[9] Cf. Kaufmann and Hassemer (2002), p. 34.

phase (end of the twentieth century and beginning of the twenty-first century), it was marked by a *crisis of meaning*, which was responsible for the loss of innovation and ability to respond to the contemporary challenges of Law. It is important that this third phase be understood, since it is the current state of the *General Theory of Law* as it is perceived: (1) a loss of discursive repercussion in the midst of other *legal discourses* of doctrine; (2) a theoretical routine of reproducing concepts, failing to respond to the effective needs of self-reflection on Law; (3) a repetition of ready-made formulas, which make use of concepts that are outdated; (4) the use of abstractions divorced from contextual experience; (5) a disconnection with the transformations of the present time, revealed by the inability to incorporate the thematization of current challenges of the self-understanding of Law.

And, in fact, while the *curricular content*, *teaching methods*, and *didactic discourse* about the discipline of the *General Theory of Law* have petrified some legal categories, fixed on the basis of conceptual achievements made in the past, the social dynamics have undermined their bases of understanding. Resynchronizing the stability of the discipline with achievements of the present time is now an imperative for the effective and reflective exercise that the discipline proposes. For this reason, the *General Theory of Law* has been challenged to transform itself, to the extent of the changes in Law in recent decades—which were not present at the time of the emergence of the *General Theory of Law*—, having a deep impact on legal knowledge, due to a number of factors, such as: (1) the proliferation of *General Theories of Specialities*; (2) the explosion of the emergence of new branches of Law (*Digital Law*; *Bio Doctrinal Law*; *Climate Disaster Law*; *Animal Rights*); (3) the consolidation of *Common Law* of Economic Blocs, the example of European Law; (4) the intensification of the interdisciplinary dialogue between the *Normative Sciences of Law* and fields of knowledge parallel to legal knowledge (the example of the relationship between *Medicine* and *Law*, in *Bio Doctrinal Law*; the example of the relationship between *Electronic Engineering* and *Law*, in *Digital Law*); (5) the constitutionalization of the branches of Law; (6) the emergence of new areas of legal knowledge[10]; (7) the proliferation of *Statutes* (*Statute of the Elderly*; *Statute of Persons with Disabilities*; *Youth Statute*), which gravitate around the *Civil Code*, accentuating the perception of "decoding" legislation; (8) the introduction of new techniques for resolving antinomies (the example of the technique of dialogue of legal juridical sources and the technique of weighting); (9) the growing imbrication between *Domestic Law* and *International Law*, in the light of globalization; (10) the principialization of Law, admitting that the legal system is made up of legal rules and legal principles; (11) the hybridization of the *common law* and *civil law* systems, through a more intense reciprocal coexistence of their institutes, the example of the expansion of the use of *judicial precedents* in *civil law*.

In these terms, the challenges currently posed on renewing the understanding within the *General Theory of Law* are not small. Insofar as the *General Theory of*

[10] "An 'area of law' only exists, then, if it is intersubjectively recognised to exist by the 'legal complex', or some important subset of this, in a given Society" (Khaitan and Steel 2023, p. 80).

Law will become obsolete in its ability to offer answers to the challenges of the time, it is not without reason that it is accused of being an area marked by a merely *formalizing* approach to Law, as David Enoch does, in his provocative article entitled *Is General Jurisprudence Interesting?*.[11] Moreover, the *General Theory of Law* is accused of being marked by a strong perspective of *anachronism*, revealing in this a criticism that points to a *lack of relevance*. It has been evaluated as an instrument for understanding Law that is outdated, as being questionable in its current usefulness. Critical voices show how much the *General Theory of Law* has become a problematic field. And this can be seen from the perspective not of an isolated group of jurists, but many jurists who have wondered about this, regardless of whether they are from the tradition of *common law*, or even, from the tradition of *continental law*.[12]

2.2 *The General Theory of Law: Modern Discourse, Guiding Myth and Paradigm Crisis*

Since the collapse of *modern discourse*, as much in *Science* in general, as in the *Science of Law*—taking in *modern discourse* as a form of historical expression that gave birth to *scientism*, which values a specialized, analytical, methodical, formalist, and purist *discourse*—, the *crisis of meaning* has been demonstrating the limits in how to understand *Science*. In particular, in the field of Law, the *crisis of meaning* will be tested as a *crisis of Law*, leading to a loss of credibility of the central paradigm that organized the way in which *modern discourse* has organized jurists' knowledge of how the legal system works. In the field of Law, it was the *model of normative positivism* by Hans Kelsen[13] that acted as a *guiding myth* for jurists.[14] Since the *discursive hegemony* crisis of this model, jurists have come to realize that the *methodological gap* was a consequence of the *crisis of a way to explain Law*. When this type of critical awareness arises, which takes into account the anomaly in the regularity of the scientific standards adopted at the time, the search for overcoming *scientific paradigms* is put in place.[15] This, one of the responses to the *state of crisis* in the *General Theory of Law* has been the *methodological revision* and *diversification in the lines of analysis*, opening up a plurality of perspectives and new lines of analysis. In this map of renewal, we find dedicated theorists of concepts as much varied as they are divergent. And renewal has meant achieving a more robust

[11] "A provocative way of putting my conclusion is that general jurisprudence is not that interesting" (Enoch 2015, p. 01).

[12] See Blalock (2014), p. 78; Dickson (2017), p. 20; Ost and Kerchov (2002); Delmas-Marty (2004), p. 46.

[13] Cf. Kelsen (2000), p. 235.

[14] "La soi-disant 'théorie pure' du droit s'avère donc elle aussi tributaire d'un grand récit fondateur" (Ost 2004, p. 34).

[15] *Vide* Kuhn (2003), pp. 78 and 95.

capacity to meet the demands of self-criticism the in the field of formulating *theoretical discourse* about *legal discourse*.

In these terms, the *crisis of meaning* is overcome through the tasks of self-criticism by jurists, about their practices. But, this still does not produce an unanimity as to the *function* to be attributed to the *General Theory of Law*. According to Italian theorist Alfonso Cattania, in his work *Manuale di teoria generale del diritto* (1998), a current *General Theory of Law* for today's times should focus on the study of *general notions* (*nozioni generali*),[16] provided it is relativized in time and history. And, in turn, according to Italian theorist Riccardo Guastini, in his work *Delle fonti a lle norme* (1990), the *General Theory of Law* would not be able to provide general notions for all legal systems, therefore adopting the idea of *General Theory of Law*, in a weak sense, to designate the study of common notions to the various branches of an empirically studied Positive Law.[17] Even if one is faced with a *soft* version of the scope of the *Theory*, it still represents a side of work that has not yet been exhausted, needing to be better positioned, whether in terms of practice, dogmatics, or in its place in face of the challenges of a global law.

2.3 The General Theory of Law: Advanced Post, Discursive Legitimacy and Technified Meaning

The state of crisis of the *General Theory of Law* is a consequence of the epistemic collapse of *Legal Positivism*—and, with this, of its explanatory capacity for the challenges of contemporary Law—, followed by its progressive replacement by the theories of *Post-positivism*. In these, the need for a new way of thinking is embedded even to the way in which the general structure of the legal system is conceived. In historical terms, it has been quite some time since the group of values that guided the Kelsenian *pyramid model* of describing the legal system (hierarchy, coherence, security, stability, and obedience) has been questioned, in view of the group of values that guide the *network model* of describing the legal system (network, creativity, lightness, pluralism, and permanent learning).[18] Jurists have come to recognize that the metaphor of the *Kelsenian pyramid*—as a mirror of the hierarchy and clarity of the distribution of legal sources among themselves—is no longer capable of describing the reality of contemporary Law.[19] In these terms, contemporary jurists experience a perception of a *cognitive vacuum* in the self-understanding of the legal system, the immediate effect of which is an increase in insecurity when dealing with legal problems.

---

[16] Cf. Catania (2010), p. 06.

[17] Cf. Guastini (2005), p. 378.

[18] *Vide* Ost and Kerchov (2002), p. 18.

[19] Cf. Delmas-Marty (2004), p. 86.

But, there is no denying, the question of the crisis of the *General Theory of Law* has to do with the perpetual state of *crisis of identity* that has always demarcated the work in this area of legal knowledge, in that it is a theoretical form of knowledge that works in the face of a mostly practical world.[20] In these terms, the crisis of the *General Theory of Law* is, on one hand, and, in part, a reflection of the transitional nature of postmodern context, from which a state of the decline of its function can be sensed.[21] In this line of reasoning, given the historical nature of the problem, the (local) crisis would be a reflection of the (general) crisis of *Philosophy*[22]—which is neither consummated, nor annulled, nor surpassed—, something that implies the (historical) crisis of *modern reason*.[23] But, beyond this, and, on the other hand, the crisis of the *General Theory of Law* must be understood, in our times, above all, as a symptom of the increased complexity in contemporary society, the expansion of the frontiers of the sciences, the specialized multiplication of the *Normative Sciences of Law* and, therefore, the increase in the *technified meaning* of Law.

In these terms, the crisis of the *General Theory of Law* should not dismiss it from its tasks or functions. Here, the aim is to understand it as a *crisis of meaning* of the *discursive place* of the *General Theory of Law*, in face of the challenges and transformations of the contemporary world. The *discursive place* of the *General Theory of Law* is that of an *advanced post* of legal knowledge, which should be capable of capturing the first waves of transformation, turning into changes in the method and way of understanding the legal system. From this position, of decisive importance for the quality of reflection of the area, no *anachronism* in this field can be tolerated. And this is because the problem with persisting for a long time in a state of crisis is that it increases the risk of *discursive legitimacy*, something that could jeopardize the place of an *advanced post* of legal knowledge of which the *General Theory of Law* was endowed with since its emergence in the history of the modernity of Law.

2.4 *The Discursive Place of the General Theory of Law: The Desynchronization Between the Reflexive Function and the Resolutive Function*

In fact, the *General Theory of Law* has not lost its place, function, or role, preserving its importance for the tasks of the self-understanding of the legal system. In addition to what has already been said, it is understood that the *crisis of meaning* is

---

[20] "As the theoretical wing of an intensely practical discipline, legal philosophy sometimes appears to be undergoing a perpetual identity crisis, its self-conception and aspirations unclear, even in jurisprudential writings of the highest calibre" (Dickson 2001, pp. 01–02).

[21] "In other words, the decline of legal theory is seen as another casualty of the more general death of metatheory in the postmodern era" (Blalock 2014, p. 78).

[22] *Vide* Kaufmann and Hassemer (2002), pp. 34–35.

[23] Cf. Neves (2003), pp. 9–22.

a consequence of the state of *desynchronization* between the *reflexive function* of the *General Theory of Law* and the *resolutive function* of the *Normative Sciences of Law*, to the extent that there was a contraction in the *reflexive function* in the face of the expansion of the *resolutive function*. The *reflexive function* implies a distanced look, endowed with a high degree of generality, aimed at exercising a theoretical capability for understanding phenomena, in relation to the *Normative Sciences of Law*. The *resolutive function* implies a localized look, endowed with high degree of specialization, aimed at exercising a capability for immediate application through legal practice.

In the contemporary world, due to the increase in social complexity, there has been a broadening in the universe of meaning of Law and a deepening of the branched specialization of the *Normative Sciences of Law*. Hence, the current process of modernization has brought with it the demand for legal security for increasingly specialized universes of meaning, due to the information overload of the media—in the way that Niklas Luhmann, in *Die Realität der Massenmedien*, identifies the rise of its central role in contemporary society.[24] In these terms, contemporary science coexists with an explosion of *meaning*, needing to be treated in such a way as to increase the acuity in the treatment of studied phenomena. Under these conditions, because it is endowed with a high degree of generality, the *General Theory of Law* has become the *background* of the *Normative Sciences of Law*, insofar as these are endowed with a high degree of technical speciality, to the extent of the immediate usefulness and practical operationality they provide jurists. Gradually, these are becoming the *scientific vanguard*, in the face of an *obscured and pale background*, still echoing the memories of the outdated concepts of *Legal Positivism*.

3 The Discursive Relationship Between the *General Theory of Law* and the *General Theories of Specialities*

3.1 The Science of Law: Branching, Ultra-Specialization, and Micro-Segmentation

The progress of the *Science of Law* takes place on the same basis as the progress of all *Science*. Modernity has meant a process of increasing autonomization and specialization for *Science*. *Science* broke away from *Philosophy* and *Theology*, in order to focus on the basis of scientific method. From the point of view of the *History of Law*, the historical arc from the end of the Middle Ages to Modernity implied, for the *Science of Law*, a progressive abandonment of *Canon Law* and *Roman Law*, toward the formation of a *Modern Law*. At the beginning of the nineteenth century, *Modern Law* implied the recognition of a rational, secular, positive, codified, and

[24] Cf. Luhmann (2005), pp. 16–17.

enlightened Law.[25] This environment has made it possible for the emergence of the *General Theory of Law*. In these terms, within the history of the development of *Modern Law*, the *Normative Sciences of Law* will evolve on the basis of a process of logical unfolding (general → particular), through chains of segmentation (civil law → property law → land law), implying distancing relationships between specialities (civil law → contract law → consumer law), progressively moving from general (macro; origin; foundation) to specific (micro; derived; subsequent).

The *Science of Law* is understood here as a manifestation of a *scientific discourse* about Law. It is a *mode of discourse* in circulation within the legal system, which collaborates with the cognitive tasks of Law, in the form of *specialized knowledge*. The *Science of Law* can therefore be characterized as a *legal knowledge* marked by: (1) objectivity, (2) autonomy, (3) specialization, (4) heuristics, (5) technical language, (6) interdisciplinarity, and (7) technical–scientific environment.[26] The process of the unfolding of the *Science of Law* into *new branches* (branching) implies recognizing some processes of scientification of social reality, such as: (1) expansion: broadening of horizons of understanding Law; (2) officialization: institutionalization of a new branch; (3) subdivision: specialization of the *Science of Law*; (4) unfolding: rise in the complexity of the *Science of Law*; (5) qualification: analytical refinement of scientific categories. In this sense, it is clear that the *Science of Law* progresses through *thematic subdivision* (increasing, progressive and of no return), in historical cycles and periods that accompany social transformations, in a profound relationship of implication with the evolving of the method and scientific techniques. With every change in legislation and expansion of the sectors that are an object of legislation, the more Law (and, with this, the *macro universe* of *legal meaning*) expands its horizon of understanding. The expansion of legislated Law should correspond to a natural process of expansion of the legal system. Throughout the history of the process of modernizing the *Science of Law*, jurists have been called upon to adapt legal knowledge to new realities and conjunctures.

This can be assessed, when the phases of the history of modernization of the *Science of Law* is analyzed, from the nineteenth century—accompanying, in parallel, the phases of the development of the *General Theory of Law*—, it is possible to distinguish three phases: (1) *phase of extensive Specialities*: the *Science of Law* is branched out, without losing its unity, marked by extensive specialities, so that only a jurist was capable of knowing an entire branch of Law. During this phase, among jurists, the practice of writing lengthy comments (in France, Tronchet, Portalis, Bigot de Préameneu, Maleville) on modern codes and elaborating on enormous treatises with several volumes predominated, dedicated to a single branch of Law (nineteenth century). A jurist is given the condition of knowing the totality of an entire branch, or, sometimes, the totality of the legal system; (2) *phase of restricted Specialities*: the *Science of Law* is pluralized, maintaining its unity, accommodating restricted specialities, so that jurists are no longer capable of mastering an entire

[25] Cf. Wieacker (1993), pp. 404–415.

[26] Cf. Bittar (2022a, b).

branch of Law, surrendering only to a more confined task of analyzing an internal area within a branch of Law (end of twentieth century). A jurist is given the condition of partial development of the legal system, starting from the branch in which he works; (3) *phase of fragmented Specialities*: the *Science of Law* is fragmented, on the basis of a loss of unity. In this phase, it is not by the mere *multiplication* of branches, but by the *subdivision* into increasingly more *specialized* levels and *fragmentary diversification* that the *Science of Law* progresses, in a digital environment of the intense circulation of information and profound imbrication of knowledge. The horizontal nature of the network, the plurality of sources, the acceleration of the circulation of information, generates a *cognitive deficit* in the ability to unify knowledge. In this phase, among jurists, there is such pluralism that the branches are lost in their reciprocal connections, generating a perception of an entropic chaos of information, with a loss of unity in understanding the whole legal system (beginning of the twenty-first century). A jurist is not even given the condition to completely know the branch of activity in which he or she works.

In the context of the society of information, this last phase implies the huge explosion in the circulation of data, the systematic practice of interdisciplinarity, the integrative circulation of various types of knowledge and the growing accumulation of scientific databases. Among jurists, the impact of this new context for the *Science of Law* has meant the task of dealing with: (1) *overcrowding*: the exorbitant increase in the volume of legal information in circulation; (2) *thickening*: the increase in the density of legal information in circulation; (3) a *complexification*: the increase in the complexity in the correlation between legal and social information; (4) *segmentation*: the increase in the segmentation of legal information in circulation, even leading to *micro-segmentation*. Thus, the *Science of Law* of our times is practiced on the basis of *ultra-specialization* (special knowledge about an increasing smaller portion of legal knowledge) and *micro-segmentation* (the subdivision of smaller parts of legal knowledge into highly branched trees of knowledge). To the extent that *legal knowledge* is impacted by these conditions, jurists' perception that it is possible to know and master the whole legal system has become increasingly impossible. In this sense, jurists' *topical vision* becomes an impediment to a *general vision* of the legal system.

3.2 The General Theory of Law and the General Theories of Specialities: A General Discursive Logic and a Local Discursive Logic

The increase in social complexity leads legislation toward an expansion in the multiplication of normative texts and an increase in the density of the universe of the meaning of Law. The *Normative Sciences of Law* capture these changes, *recodifying-them* in the form of *new knowledge*. As a result, increasingly refined categories of analysis are produced. The perception of the absence of *general knowledge* engenders a consequence to creating the *General Theories* of the *Normative Sciences of Law*, or even, the *General Theories* of the *Specialities* of Law. From an exceptional and reduced use, in recent times, a proliferation of the *General Theories* has been perceived. This phenomenon points to the need to introduce *general discursive logic* in the scope of a field marked by *local discursive logic*.

And, in fact, this has been perceived as a movement to reorganize legal knowledge on two levels. On a first level, the formation of *General Theory* of an integral branch of Law, which offers a system of elementary concepts on dogmatics and its main institutes (*General Theory of Procedure*; *General Theory of Civil Law*; *General Theory of Administrative Law*). On a second level, the formation of *General Theory* of parts of a segmented branch of Law (*General Theory of Legal Business*; *General Theory of Evidence and Proof*; *General Theory of Appeals*; *General Theory of Civil Liability*). Based on this double movement of reorganization, it is a question of identifying that there are two levels of deepening in which the need for the *generalization* of thematic content is perceived.

Undoubtedly, the emergence of the *General Theories of Specialities* is a contemporary phenomenon. But, their roots arise from the traditional division of *modern Codes*—for *Civil Law*, from *German Civil Code* (BGB, 1900), and for Penal Law, from *Codex Iuris Bavarici Criminalis* (1751, *Bavarian Penal Code*)[27]—into a *General Part* (unity and coherence; a way of using specific rules; a form of rationalizing the private system of law; a repository of general rules of law) and a *Special Part* (a repository of special rules of private law; specific rules). And, above this division, another subdivision is the formation of a *General Theory of the General Part* and a *General Theory of the Special Part*.[28] Be that as it may, currently, a return to the *status quo ante* before the division between *General Part* and *Special Part* is unthinkable for the branches of *codified Law*, as this *summa diviso* has been incorporated definitively into the scientific conception that one has of Law.

Thus, increasingly, what is apparent is that the *General Part* of a specialized branch implies the need to insert a *reflexive function* into a field endowed with a *resolutive function*. Here is the manifestation of a response linked to the *search for meaning* in the branched use of Law. *Local discursive logic* is enriched with the addition of a *general discursive logic* (specialized generalization). This adaptation to historical transformations of current Law is a clear *sign of insufficiency* of the isolated use of the *resolutive function* of legal dogmatics (traditionally divorced from the *reflexive function*). Now, it is seen that the insertion of a *reflexive function* (localized and branched) once again provides the specialized, technical, and dogmatic branch of Law with a *local meaning* connected to a *general meaning*, something that looks to respond to the challenges that arise from the loss of perception of the *general meaning* of the legal system.

---

[27] Cf. Gomes (2012), pp. 28–32.

[28] Cf. Gomes (2012), pp. 223 and ss.

3.3 The Stripping of the Discursive Place of the General Theory of Law: Unicity, Plurality, and Federative Relationship

Here, it can also be seen that the emergence of the *General Theories of Specialities* is a reflection of the *void* left by the collapse of *Legal Positivism* in the scope of the *General Theory of Law*. In any case, this is something that cannot be regretted or criticized, as it is something that has already been irreversibly incorporated into contemporary practices of the *Science of Law*. Thus, gone are the days when it was possible to talk about the *unicity* of the *General Theory of Law*, in the face of the diverse specialized branches of Law, to the extent that it currently has the task of coexisting with the *plurality of the General Theories of Specialities*.

In any case, this relationship of coexistence is based on a complementary reciprocity. The *General Theory of Law* needs the *General Theories of* Specialities, and cannot be put in its place, as these reflect *local discursive logic* (applicable to the set of provisions of a branch of Law), while the former reflects a *general discursive logic* (applicable to the set of provisions of all branches of Law). While the former is the expression of an analytically extensive *scientific discourse*, these are expressions of an analytically sectorial *scientific discourse*. In turn, the *General Theories of Specialities* need the *General Theory of Law*, as they are insufficiently "general" for the level of demand of a *General Theory of Law*, which confers *unicity* to the integrating experience of legal knowledge.

But, one could question whether the *plurality* of the *General Theories of Specialities* has not quite been suffocating and, also, stripping the *discursive place* of the *General Theory of Law*. The state of affairs points to the idea of a *generalization* that occurs in branches of Law, which means that the development of a *local general vision* ends up *consuming* a little of the idea of the *extensiveness* of the *General Theory of Law*, corroding the previous space of *reflexive exclusivity* that the *General Theory of Law* has maintained with all branches of Law. In this sense, one must question if, by associating the *reflexive function* to the *resolutive function*, the *General Theories of Specialities* have not ended up reducing the field of expression of the *General Theory of Law*.

But, contrary to the thesis of the stripping the *discursive place* of the *General Theory of Law*, the aim here is to support the thesis that this maintains a *federative relationship* with the *General Theories of Specialities*. Its current task is that of conglomerating the *General Theories of Specialities*. And this is because the *General Theory of Law* performs a more extensive function than that exercised by the *General Theories of Specialities*, which, often, are supplied with *macro-concepts* originating from that, in order to deal with the local problems and challenges of the branches of Law. In these terms, an updated view of the issue in question, it must be understood that we are dealing with a *General Theory* of the *Special Theories*. Figure 1 seeks to portray this idea.

Hence, the relationship between the *General Theory of Law* and the *General Theories of Specialities* is that of *reflexive cooperation*, which is discussed as

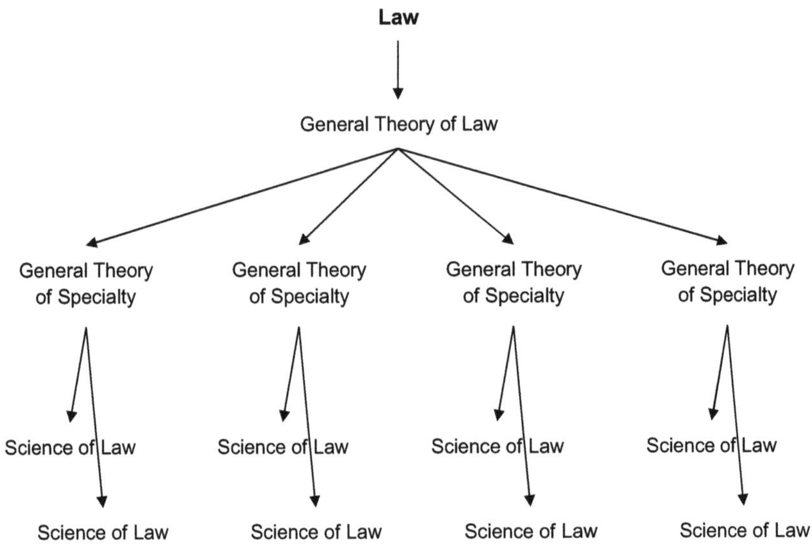

Fig. 1 Diagram showing the federative relationship between the *General Theory of Law* and the *General Theories of Specialities*

follows: (1) the *General Theory of Law* maintains the *cognitive unity* of the entire legal system, so as to supply the *Special Theories* with the set of omni comprehensive categories of Law; this means that, in its abstraction, it can no longer proceed alone and isolated, but in a state of dialogue with the areas specialized by their transformations (the local transformations modify the very internal design of the *General Theory of Law*); (2) the *General Theories of Specialities* point out to the *General Theory of Law* the interpretative problems of a specific branch and transform the comprehensive understanding that the *General Theory of Law* has with the branches. If Law as a whole is in motion, the more a segmented area increases in complexity and speciality, the greater the tendency to adopt a *General Theory of Speciality*.

4 Discursive Polyglotism and the Oniabrangency of the *General Theory of Law*

4.1 General Theory of Law: The Cyclopean View of Law

The *General Theory of Law* offers a *meta-level* of conceptual, systematic, and abstract understanding, dedicated to understanding the legal system as a unit. It is a *scientific discourse* that implies an *oniabrangency* approach to Law. Following Jean-Louis Bergel's opinion closely, in his work *Théorie Générale de Droit*, the

General Theory of Law studies the "globality" of legal order.[29] The role of the *General Theory of Law* is to provide the theoretical support that allows for a view of the whole, capable of optimizing the practical application of Law.[30] Finally, the *General Theory of Law*, in Joseph Raz's view, must be able to state what Law means.[31] Furthermore, for this task to be possible, the *General Theory of Law* is developed on the basis of a *discursive polyglotism*—understood as a faculty of *interdiscursive translation*, capable of promoting cognitive dialogue, and, as a result, absorb knowledge from different matrices—without which it would not be able to develop *interdisciplinary transit*, a condition for its epistemic task. In these terms, the *General Theory of Law* implies: (1) an extensive study of legal order; (2) an advanced post for observing the development of Law; (3) a source of interpretation and organization in the way Positive Law is expressed; (4) a mobilization of debates and opinions that reinforce the critical, reflexive, and rationalizing place of Law, and (5) a field of work marked by evaluative judgments.[32]

By putting the *General Theory of Law* in its *epistemic place*, i.e., in front of the immense territory of Law, one could even use this metaphor of the *cyclopean view*. The *cyclopean view* implies an *archipelago view*. The *General Theory of Law* takes the territory of Law as an undivided whole, within a *global and unitary vision* of the immensity of disciplines into which Law is subdivided. It seeks to offer a systemization of fundamental categories (concept of law, norm, system, interpretation, application, decision) for understanding Law, whose function is to provide an *oni-abrangent vision*, indispensable and complementary for other technical and specialized tasks contained in the *Normative Sciences of Law*. Considering the reflexive ability to transit above and beyond the *Normative Sciences of Law*, the *General Theory of Law* is capable of offering them the *macro-concepts* of common use and interest to all other disciplines. The *General Theory of Law* understands its object based on the preselection of *macro-concepts* in the face of *microconcepts*. *Macro-concepts* are those that: (1) are important for the understanding and general functioning of the legal system; (2) crossover and involve all the specific branches of the *Science of Law*, which, because they are dedicated to *microconcepts*, cannot deal with them; (3) form a set of problems-type, normally addressed by the *General Theory of Law*; (4) are extensive concepts, with a high level of internal technicity to the culture of Law, having a theoretical–analytical nature. In turn, the *Normative Sciences of Law* take the territory of Law as a whole subdivided into *Specialities*. The *Normative Sciences of Law* are committed to a reduced dimension and seek to

[29] Cf. Bergel (2006), p. 13.

[30] *Vide* Larenz (1983), pp. 277–278. In the same perspective, see also: "En ce sens, la théorie du droit ne peut être que la théorie de la pratique du droit" (Moor 2010, p. 06).

[31] "Therefore, as here understood, a theory of law provides an account of the nature of law. The thesis I will be defending is that a theory of law is successful if it meets two criteria: First, it consists of propositions about the law which are *necessarily* true, and second, they explain what the law is" (Raz 2011, p. 17).

[32] "Accordingly, let us consider some prominent arguments for thinking that legal theory must be inherently evaluative in nature" (Marmor and Sarch 2019: online).

describe the state of development of a specific branch of Positive Law. Unable to transcend the boundaries of their specialities, they end up exercising a *specialized view*. The *specialized view* implies an *insular vision*.

In this sense, from its *discursive place*, the *General Theory of Law* corresponds to a theorization about the positivity of Law, methodically constructed in a way to be doubly tied in opposite directions: (1) tied to the *concrete*, since it is from Positive Law as *concrete data* that it draws its starting point, from an inductive perspective; (2) tied to the *abstract*, since it does not stick to *phenomenal concreteness*, exercising an epistemological attitude of one who hovers over the reality of Positive Law, from a deductive perspective. It is, therefore, the most abstract dimension of the *Science of Law*, to use the words of Antônio Castanheira Neves.[33] In these terms, the *General Theory of Law* maintains different relationships of proximity in relation to: (1) *Normative Sciences of Law*: the relationship is one of proximity through normativity (the legal norm as a center of scientific investigation) and abstractive distance through method (the specialized norm as a focus of work); (2) *Philosophy of Law*: the relationship is one of proximity through method (the theoretical reflection as a center of investigation), distance due to level of abstraction in the problematic treatment of the concept of justice (the concept of justice and problematization of the horizons of justice as a focus of work).

The collaboration for the practical and technical refinement of the legal system is one of the greatest contributions of the *General Theory of Law*. And this is precisely because its task is not only *parochial*, but *extensive* and *universalist*, as the position of William Twining rightly postulates.[34] It has the ability, by its abstraction, to make theoretical concepts transcend to the local origin, generating the theoretical–scientific dialogue that is specific to the globalized scientific community. It is a fact that the *General Theory of Law* has allowed for the approximate theoretical dialogue of different legal systems. In this sense, the *General Theory of Law* is a facet of the study of Law that transcends the positivity of local Law, allowing for shared advances in legal knowledge from a global perspective.[35] With this, it can be seen that the *General Theory of Law*: (1) shares similar generalities that are specific to the *abstract form* of Law; (2) does not share unspecific particularities that are specific to the *local knowledge* of Law; (3.) but, in some cases, it may import techniques and solutions from other legal orders, with adaptations that will be absorbed according to the efforts and task of jurists that find themselves in the target realities. As a result, the *General Theory of Law* implies a common and convergent effort, global and synchronic, dialogic and polemic, seeking to advance the understanding of Law and that points to the progress of Positive Law.

---

[33] Cf. Neves (2003), p. 31.

[34] "Similar considerations apply to the term 'general jurisprudence' as to the over use of 'global'. 'General' in this context has at least four different meanings: (a) abstract, as in "théorie générale du droit"; (b) universal, at all times in all places; (c) widespread, geographically or over time; (d) more than one, up to infinity" (Twining 2005, p. 654).

[35] "Our discipline has never been entirely local and it is becoming more cosmopolitan" (Twining 2005, p. 670).

4.2 *The General Theory of Law: Narrativity, Diegesis, and Constituent Discourse*

As we have already seen, the *General Theory of Law* is a *theoretical–analytical discourse* on *legal discourse*. Insofar as the universe of meaning of Law has its own postulates and operates on the basis of internal logic, the *General Theory of Law* seeks to *apprehend-them* and *describe-them*. Thus, its approach to the legal system is *diegetic*, since it is involved in the *reality specific* to *legal narrativity*. It is committed to: (1) the self-understanding of the legal system; and (2) the reflexive resolution of operational problems inherent in the practice of Law. In addition, the *General Theory of Law* can be taken, also, as a *constituent discourse* (*discours constituant*) for the self-description of the legal system.[36]

Precisely for this reason, the *enunciative status* of *theoretical–philosophical discourse* is endowed with particular discursive authority. It is a *discourse* that is above other discourses (the discourse of legal dogmatics), which guides all operations of the legal system (the discourse of legal practice) and, above all, that is descriptive of the entirety of activities carried out by the legal system (a meta-comprehensive discourse). In these terms, it is a *founding discourse* and *not founded*, which aims to offer general benchmarks of legal thinking. It is a *discourse* that brings jurists together, and, therefore, a specialized discourse aimed at specialists, who need to find a *common point* (theoretical–reflexive), founded on *theoretical–scientific rationality*, taking it as a goal for the exercise of its tasks.

It is specific to the theory, because of the distance it takes from the practice, *to enunciate* the *meaning* of Law with the support of scientific method and based on analytical perspectives. In these terms, Law is in search for a *meaning of its own*, which can be produced from a *narrative of its own*. The task of the *General Theory of Law* is, therefore, to offer a *narrative of its own* that functions as a field of isolation for work of jurists. Following François Ost's reflection closely, in his work *Raconter la loi*, it can be seen that Hans Kelsen's *Pure Theory of Law*—as a historical example of the manifestation of *modern discourse* in the field of the *General Theory of Law*—was capable of providing the *récit fondateur* necessary for a rational, methodological, and substantiated explanation, capable of providing the scientific autonomy required for the whole scope of the *Science of Law*.[37] So, as we can see, *narrativity* is at the heart of *theoretical discourse* on *legal discourse*.

---

[36] Cf. Maingueneau (2008a, b), p. 47.

[37] For a criticism of this theoretical perspective made by François Ost, see: "La soi-disant 'théorie pure' du droit s'avère donc elle aussi tributaire d'un grand récit fondateur" (Ost 2004, p. 34).

5 Theoretical Discourse and the Metalanguage of the General Theory of Law

5.1 The Enunciation of Scientific Discourse: The Language of Reason and Truth Effect

Enunciation is an *act of language*—closely following the concept of *enunciation* (*énonciation*, fr.) developed by Algirdas Julien Greimas and Joseph Courtés, in *Dictionnaire*—,[38] being responsible for the passage of the virtuality of *language-system* (*langue*) into the actuality of *discourse-speech* (*parole*). *Scientific statements* originate from the enunciative activity of scientists, which presupposes the exercise of *veridiction* (*véridiction*).[39] In the line of Greimasian understanding,[40] the *act of enunciation* of *scientific discourse* presupposes scientific research, which qualifies as being a *cognitive activity* (*activité cognitive*) that is carried out around a *program* (*program*), marked by a set of *deontic precautions* (*précautions déontiques*), by rules of producing knowledge, which results in the act of scientific publication (*faire-savoir*), a submission of *scientific statements* to the knowledge of the *scientific community*. In this sense, fulfilling its social function, *scientific statements* are usually the bearers of *scientific discoveries*, and, in this, lies the progress of *Science* and its commitment to transforming consciousness and understanding of the world.

Scientific enunciation is the activity specific to the *discursive genre* of *Science* and, for this reason, it is linked to a series of characteristics that are inherent to them, which are: (1) the *enunciative shifting out* (*débrayage*, fr.) of the enunciator; (2) the *truth effect* on scientific discourse; (3) the unfolding of a *methodological status*; (4) the use of a *terminologized language*. The ideal that demarcates the formation of *scientific discourse* is that it is the fruit of *objectivity*, *neutrality*, *impartiality*, *descriptiveness*, and *veracity*. In this way, *scientific discourse* is normally produced from a process of *scientific enunciation* in which the *enunciator* disappears, leaving behind only *highly guaranteed statements of scientificity*. This process is the *enunciative shifting out* that produces the *effect of the meaning of objectivity* of *scientific discourse* as a result.[41]

Scientific discourse presupposes a series of constraints in order to be expressed through *scientific statements*. The problematization from this point is very clear in the chapter *Du discours scientifique en Sciences Sociales*, in the work *Sémiotique et Sciences Sociales*, by Algirdas Julien Greimas.[42] This is where it can be read that *scientific discourse* seeks a form of expression that uses *linguistic procedures* that

[38] Cf. Greimas and Courtés (1993), pp. 123–126, entry *énoncé* e *énonciation*.

[39] Cf. Greimas (1976a, b), p. 66.

[40] Cf. Greimas and Courtés (1993), p. 322, entry *scientificité*.

[41] Cf. Fiorin (2016), p. 39.

[42] Cf. Greimas (1976a, b), p. 36.

guarantee completeness and veracity.[43] *Scientific communication (faire-savoir)* is a particular challenge for all *Science*, implying specializations and procedures of *scientific validation. Scientific validation* implies that every *scientific enunciation* can and should be subjected to careful analysis and verification, given that there is no *Science* without *falseability* of scientific results.[44] This way, in the Greimasian line of analysis, it can be said that *scientific discourse* presupposes, on one hand, a *persuasive doing (faire persuasif)* of the enunciator and, on the other hand, an *interpretative doing (faire intérprétatif)* of the enunciatee.

5.2 *The Scientific Statements of the General Theory of Law: Language of Description and Methodological Language*

The *scientific statements* of the *General Theory of Law* are not just any *linguistic enunciations*. They are *scientific statements* situated in a universe of knowledge, within the field of *Human and Social Sciences*.[45] In these terms, the *General Theory of Law* corresponds to the part of the *Science of Law* responsible for formulating *general theoretical statements* capable of describing the way the legal system works. For this reason, theorists of Law are not lesser scientists than other social scientists, obeying the same cognitive canons of *Social Sciences*,[46] with the particularity that its scientific object is the universe of legal norms. As a result, it can be understood that the *General Theory of Law* is not a *General Theory of social action*, specific to the field of Law, thus having a markedly *nomological* nature.[47]

In addition, it should be said that the *scientific statements* of the *General Theory of Law* differ from other modalities, due to the fact that, first and foremost, *theoretical statements*, which presuppose the analysis of what the field of scientific exercise of the *theory* (*theoría*, gr.) is. The examples of the *scientific statements* of the *General Theory of Law* are many ("The legal system is an open system"; "Every legal norm is interpretable"; "Validity is the formal belonging of the norm to the legal system"). In this sense, accompanying Greimasian analysis, it can be said that the *theory* presupposes "...a coherent set of hypotheses susceptible of being

---

[43] "Pour éliminer ces malentendus et rendre le savoir qui se construit transmissible, le discours scientifique fait alors siennes toutes les procédures linguistiques permattant de garantir la communication aussi complete et aussi véridique que possible, procédures qui relèvent d'um *savoir-faire* portant sur le *faire-savoir*" (Greimas 1976a, b, p. 36).

[44] "Every genuine test of a theory is an attempt to falsify it, or to refute it. Testability is falsifiability; but there are degrees of testability: some theories are more testable, more exposed to refutation, than others; they take, as it were, greater risks" (Popper 2000, pp. 33–39).

[45] "Théorie intégrée dans les autres sciences sociales, au même titre qu'elles: elle est aussi une science sociale (...)" (Moor 2010, p. 305).

[46] *Vide* Habermas (2005).

[47] *Vide* Habermas (2005), pp. 63–64.

submitted to verification…," as can be read in *Dictionnaire*.[48] In its internal process of construction, the *theory* implies the hierarchization of concepts, categories, and definitions, which ends up resulting in a coherent whole, forming a system of ideas capable of providing an explanation for a particular phenomenon studied. In its development, the *theory* presupposes the formulation of a *language of description* (*langage de description*), in relation to *object-Law*, and a *methodological language* (*langage méthodologique*), in relation to the set of scientific suppositions that substantiate the approach of *object-Law*.[49]

Above all, it is a type of *enunciation* demarked by a *theoretical–philosophical* status, which implies a textual capacity for the elaboration and concatenation of *theoretical–philosophical concepts*, given that, in Cossutta's perspective of analysis, concepts are nothing more than *operators of generalization* (*operáteur de généralisation*).[50] And it is from this that the *General Theory of Law* draws its most central property and mark of distinction, in that it marks itself out as *conceptual* and *abstract knowledge*, which reflects on the *empiricism* and *experience of Law*, now taken at a simply theorized level of comprehension. The *scientific statements* of the *General Theory of Law* presuppose that all *legal experience* and the countless set of *legal acts* practiced in a particular society are condensed there, at a high abstract level, with loss of empiricism, and projected on the basis of veritable, theoretical, and verifiable statements.

5.3 *The Scientific Statements of the General Theory of Law: Quality, Description, and Distinction*

This allows us to affirm that the *scientific enunciations* of the *General Theory of Law* are marked by a series of qualities, which allow them to be distinguished from others. In this line of question, the aim is to identify, elaborate, and present the ten qualities that are characteristic of this modality of *scientific discourse*, which are discussed as follows: (1) *universal statements*: they are of universal scope because they are capable of generating understanding, analysis, and global theoretical dialogues, bearing mind the relativism and historicism of legal systems; (2) *abstract statements*: they are abstract because they are detached from the concrete themes of Positive Law; (3) *empirical–analytical statements*: they are drawn from empirical experience, regularity of normative phenomena and systematic observation of legal practice; (4) *theoretical statements*: they supply the *reflexive function* of the *Science of Law*, implying a meta-understanding of legal experience, connecting theory and

---

[48] "On entend habituellement par théorie um ensemble cohérent d'hypothèses, susceptibles d'être soumises à la vérification (…)" (Greimas and Courtés 1993, p. 394, verbete *théorie*).

[49] Cf. Greimas and Courtés (1993), p. 395, verbete *théorie*.

[50] "Certes *le concept est un opérateur de généralisation*, um facteur d'abstraction, au moins sous la forme dominante dans l'historie de la philosophie" (Cossutta 2020, p. 18).

practice; (5) *rational and demonstrable statements*: they are based on the ability to describe a nomological reality and imply rational justification to scientific reasoning; (6) *complex statements*: they refer to various statements (doctrinal, normative, jurisprudential, scientific, philosophical), with the ability to analyze them and conglomerate them, with the aim to produce a comprehensive understanding of the way the legal system works; (7) *unifying statements*: they make a general view of the legal system possible based on its capacity to descriptively unify all legal knowledge and the ways in which the legal system operates; (8) *general statements*: they form a *general language*, as a *nonspecialized language* in the area of Law, detached from the specialities and *Normative Sciences of Law*; (9) *polemic statements*: they are constituted within academic debate, in the midst of trends and traditions, being subject to criticism, reevaluation, and polemic discussion; (10) *argumentative statements*: they are capable of providing the reasons that support ideas and concepts, aimed at convincing readers.

In this way, the *General Theory of Law* forms a field of *knowledge* focused on the problematizing self-understanding of *legal meaning*,[51] being capable of adding scientific progress in its field of work, whenever it is able to: (1) formulate a new methodological concept capable of providing a reasonable explanation on the nature of Law and the way the legal system works; (2) identify new problems and the way to deal with its issues; (3) develop criticism on the predominant theoretical paradigms. This shows that *theoretical–philosophical knowledge* does not imply a solipsistic cognitive act, insofar as—following the concept developed by Dominique Maingueneau's *Analyse du Discours*[52]—*theoretical–philosophical discourse* is demarcated in the midst of practices, institutions, and discourses, presupposing, in this way, three dimensions: (1) a *network of apparatuses* (*réseau d'appareils*, fr.), which projects the *discourse* within the framework of a institutionality that makes some speakers and others listeners, some adversaries, and others adjuvants; (2) a field (*champ*, fr.), which implies a boundary of confrontation with other doctrines, through special languages endowed with their own vocabulary; (3) an *archive* (*archive*, fr.), which makes it possible to identify where this specific *discourse* is placed in history, in the face a collective and long-standing memory of formative traditions in the area.[53]

The scientific progress achieved here shows that there is a *previous state* and a *later state* of the *General Theory of Law*, which makes us realize that it is not constructed in isolation, as it implies a construction of a subject (S1) in face of the other (S2), implying *inter-discourse* (S1 ⇔ S2). The notion of *inter-discourse* says how much *discourse* is not inscribed in a vacuum, but indeed within a set of historical relationships of a time. This relationship of implication makes it possible to verify that *theoretical–philosophical discourse* is inscribed in the world, considering a

---

[51] "Pour autant que les sciences sociales procèdent de manière normativement analytique, eles aussi ignorent la problématique de la compréhension du sens" (Habermas 2005, p. 119).

[52] Cf. Maingueneau (2020).

[53] Cf. Maingueneau (2020), pp. 201–202.

discursive universe—the discursive formations of a time—, a *discursive field*—the discourses in conflict at a given time, and a *discursive space*—the relevant questions thematized by the discourse.[54] Thus, by measuring *theoretical discourse* in relation to this multiplicity of *interdiscursive* facets, it is possible to analyze how much a *theory* is built on the basis of a tradition, inscribed in a line of thinking, opposed to a group of other concepts, distanced from many others and closed off (more or less) to the variety of the stock of knowledge of its time.

5.4 Metascientific Legal Language: A Quadruple Isotopy

When it comes to analyzing *legal discourse*, it should be borne in mind that *discourse* specific to the *General Theory of Law* is—among the *modalities of legal discourse*—,[55] the modality of *scientific discourse*, more specifically, *metascientific discourse*.[56] As with any manifestation of *metalanguage* (*métalangage*, fr.), stating that there is a *metadiscourse* presupposes, first and foremost, recognizing the existence of *linguistic levels*, elaborated and developed from the presupposition of *language-object* (*langage-objet*, fr.).[57] *Metascientific discourse* has this four-fold characteristic: (1) it is a discourse about scientific discourse; (2) it is discourse about legislative discourse; (3) it is a discourse about decision-making discourse; (4) it is a discourse about bureaucratic discourse. It is a *meta-reported discourse* on different dimensions of forms of expression of Law (Law-science, Law-legislation, Law-decision, Law-bureaucracy).

And, in fact, closely following the analysis of *legal discourse*, undertaken by Jerzy Wroblewski, in his article *Les langages juridiques*, a distinction can be made between: (1) *legal language* (*langage legal*—LL); (2) *jurisprudential legal language* (*langage juridique jurisprudentiel*—LJJ); (3) *scientific legal language* (*langage juridique scientifique*—LJS); (4) *common legal language* (*langage juridique commun*—LJC). It is from these categories that it is possible to identify the one that is specific to the *Science of Law*, which is *scientific legal language* (LJS).[58] *Scientific legal language*, is subdivided into two genres: (1) *dogmatic legal language* (*langage juridique dogmatique*—LJD); (2) *theoretical legal language* (*langage juridique théorique*—LJT).[59] The latter, *theoretical legal language* (LJT), is identified as being the one specific to the field of the *General Theory of Law*.[60]

---

[54] Cf. Maingueneau (2008a, b), pp. 33–34.

[55] Cf. Bittar (2022a, b), p. 355 and ss.

[56] *Vide* Vesting (2015), p. 36.

[57] Cf. Greimas and Courtés (1993), p. 224, entry *métalangage*.

[58] "Le *langage juridique scientifique* (LJS) est propre au discours de la science juridique" (Wroblewski 1988, p. 14).

[59] Cf. Wroblewski (1988), p. 19.

[60] "Or LJT, comme langage de la théorie du droit est strictement lié avec le contenu de la théorie" (Wroblewski 1988, p. 20).

[4th level] - *metascientific discourse* (Theory of Law - LJT)

⇓

[3rd level] - *scientific discourse* (dogmatics - LJD)

⇓

[2nd level] - *legislative discourse* (legislation - LL)

⇓

[1st level] - *referential discourse* (referent - DR)

⇓

[referential level] – *designated reality* (social reality - RD)

Fig. 2 The quadruple isotopy of metascientific discourse of the *General Theory of Law.* Created by the author, based on the ideas of Algirdas Julien Greimas and Jerzy Worbléwski

Theoretical legal language can be understood as being a *metalanguage*[61] marked by a *quadruple isotopy*, which is: (1) *theoretical legal language* (LJT), in the field of the *General Theory of Law*, it is a fourth-level *metalanguage*, in relation to the *referent world (designated reality*—RD); (2) *dogmatic legal language* (LJD) is a third-level *metalanguage*, in relation to the *referent world (designated reality*—RD)[62]; (3) *legal language* (LL) is a second-level *metalanguage*, in relation to the *referent world (designated reality*—RD); (4) *referential discourse* (DR) is a first-level *metalanguage*, in relation to the *referent world (designated reality*—RD). This *quadruple isotopy* can be seen more clearly in Fig. 2.

5.5 *The Relationship Between the General Theory of Law and the Philosophy of Law: Metalanguage of Quintuple Isotopy*

To this extent, from what has already been analyzed, we can see the high level of theoretical transcendence and abstraction in which the fields of work of the *General Theory of Law* and *Philosophy of Law* are inscribed. Closely following Eric Millard's vision, in his work *Théorie Générale du Droit*,[63] the *General Theory of Law* must be able to offer a two-sided connection, namely, on one hand, with the *Philosophy of Law* and, on the other hand, with the *Science of Law*. In the face of

[61] Cf. Wroblewski (1988), p. 20.

[62] Cf. Wroblewski (1988), pp. 17–20.

[63] "L'idée même d'une théorie du droit, partie de la philosophie du droit se donnant pour objet de permettre une Science du droit, suppose de clarifier les rapports entre Philosophie et Science d'une part, et de distinguer d'autre part la Science du droit de son objet" (Millard 2006, p. 09).

the *Philosophy of Law*, it must be able to incorporate conceptual innovations and demands for transforming the concept of justice, and, in turn, in the face of the *Science of Law*, it must be able to operate through language, the appropriate *translation* of empirical content and practical issues, raising them to the level of the more abstract demands of the *theoretical–analytical concept*. In this way, its level of concreteness and proximity to legal practice is greater, in relation to the *Philosophy of Law*, from whose higher flight supplies the possibility of renewing the concept of justice, capable of inoculating the concept of Law with a reform of practices and institutions.

To this extent, the question of a fifth level of transcendence is admitted to give way to the *Philosophy of Law*, insofar as the idea is defended here that the epistemic horizons between the *Philosophy of Law* and the *General Theory of Law* are not confused—maybe, sometimes, touching on and communicating, the reciprocal collaboration between the two domains being usual. The task of the *General Theory of Law* is not completely fulfilled when it is divorced from the screen obtained by the understanding stemming from the field of the *Philosophy of Law*, considering the divergence of trends that debate the methodological meaning of this theoretical field.[64] And, for its part, the *Philosophy of Law* does not directly touch on the *Sciences of Law*, but must mediate between the fields, through the tasks of the *General Theory of Law*.

It is to this extent that it can be considered, in the scope of Law, the *Philosophy of Law* should be taken as a *legal–reflexive discourse of apex*, implying the culmination of legal thinking, in abstraction and ability to point toward fairness, its central object being the discussion of the concept of justice. Only because it is a *discourse of apex*, the level of disengagement with the *legal form* is greater,[65] not being affiliated to *describing the legal system*, but being able to discuss it in such a way as to distance itself from its structures, to the point of being able to completely distance itself from its current foundations; with this, the dialogue with other areas of knowledge is favored, so that cognitive boundaries open up to a greater detachment from Positive Law.[66] This can be seen more closely in Fig. 3.

[5th level] - *metascientific discourse* (Philosophy of Law - LJT)

⇓

[4th level] - *metascientific discourse* (Theory of Law - LJT)

Fig. 3 The quintuple isotopy of metascientific discourse of the *Philosophy of Law*. Created by the author, based on the ideas of Algirdas Julien Greimas and Jerzy Worbléwski

[64] "There are five main families of views on this question. One view takes jurisprudence to be a form of conceptual analysis, which is to say that theories of law aim to provide an account of some concept of law" (Marmor and Sarch 2019: *online*).

[65] Cf. Del Vecchio (1979), p. 311.

[66] *Vide* Kaufmann (2002), p. 49.

5.6 *The Relationship Between the General Theory of Law and the Science of Law: The Macro-universe and the Micro-universe of Legal Meaning*

The *General Theory of Law* draws from legal dogmatics the set of concepts that have been abstracted and transformed into categories and definitions. Thus, the relationship maintained between the *General Theory of Law* and the *Normative Sciences of Law* is a relationship, on the part of the *General Theory of Law*, marked by: (1) understanding of scientific categories; (2) perception of changes and transformations; (3.) analytical–conceptual distancing; (4) detachment from utilitarian and operational nature. Now, on the part of the *Normative Sciences of Law*, it is a relationship marked by: (1) continuous replenishment of extensive vision; (2) adaptation to general conceptual parameters; (3) incorporative dialogue of extensive vision; (4) increased capacity for criticality and epistemological self-distancing. The *General Theory of Law* is, in this sense, a factor in renewing the horizons of the *Normative Sciences of Law*, informing them of their limits and deficits. It can even be said that, it acts a *sensor* in the face of the *transformations*, resulting in the ability to dynamize and renew legal knowledge, to the extent that it represents an *advanced post* of *legal knowledge*. And this, above all, due to the fact of the *high sensitivity* of the *General Theory of Law* to the modifications that have occurred in the realm of the *universe of legal meaning*.

The *General Theory of Law* works with the idea incorporated into its scientific practices that the *universe of legal meaning* is not static, but indeed a universe in motion. Since it is intertwined with *social meaning*, the transformations in social life directly affect the formation of *legal meaning*.[67] This is how it is verified, within the *universe of legal meaning*: (1) expansion in the universe of meaning of Law; (2) increase in the number of internal subsidies of branches; (3) complexification of the operational techniques of Law; (4) intensification of the dialogical exchange of information with other sectors of knowledge; (5) increase in the accumulation of knowledge, derived from *Science* and *Philosophy*; (6) change in the concept about the legal system and its way of working; (7) increase in density and normative inflation; (8) increase in the turnover of short-term normative enunciations; (9) growth in the autonomy of the *Normative Sciences of Law* to the detriment of the capacity of oniabrangency of the *General Theory of Law*.

Following the understanding of Algirdas Julien Greimas and Eric Landowski—taken from the text *Analyse sémiotique d'un discours juridique*, in *Sémiotique et Sciencies Sociales* (1976)—, the perception of the distinction of the *micro-universes of meaning* (*micro univers*) stands out.[68] From there, when distinguishing the *macro-universe* and the *micro-universe of legal meaning*, it is possible to show that these

[67] Cf. Bittar (2024a, b), pp. 159–178.

[68] "L'univers juridique étant susceptible d'une articulation en micro univers, dest le micro univers das lequal s'encadre le droit sur les sociétes commerciales qui sera visé par notre investigation" (Greimas 1976a, b, p. 87).

are associated to two levels of *codification* of *legal language*: (1) *general legal language* (LJG); (2) *specialized legal language* (LJE).[69] In these terms: (1) the *General Theory of Law* uses *general legal language* (LJG), characterized by: (1.1) *metadiscourse* about the legal system; (1.2) it has as its object the global *semantic–legal universe* in its scope; (1.3) second-level *metadiscourse* in relation to *legislative language*; (1.4) third-level *metadiscourse* in relation to *referential language*; (1.4) a predominance of theoretical–abstract concepts; (2) the *Normative Sciences of Law* use *special legal language* (LJE)—forming new areas of Law, demarcated by normative sets within the legal system, recognized intersubjectively—,[70] given that these are characterized by: (2.1) *metadiscourse* about *legal language*; (2.2) they have as their object the local *semantic–legal universe*, in their sectorial and segmented delimitation; (2.3) they operate on the basis of *specialized and technified language*; (2.4) first-level *metadiscourse* in relation to *legal language*; (2.5) second-level *metadiscourse* in relation to *referential language*; (2.6) a predominance of concepts and categories whose function is operational for legal practice.

6 The Figure of Jurist-Prometheus and Algorithmic Rationality

6.1 Automatic Enunciation and Programming Language: The Collective Actant and the Science Produced by Machines

Automatic enunciation has made another form of producing *Science* possible. The notion that the authorship of texts corresponds to *exclusive human act* has lost its place, and, currently, *automatic enunciation* (*énonciation numérique*) is increasingly establishing enhanced discursive performances (*discours numérique*)[71]—and this is valid for the generation of texts or images—,[72] mediated by new technology, in particular, by *generative Artificial Intelligence* (*generative AI*). It is to this extent that, from a post-dualist approach, it is possible to identify *automatic writing* as part of the relationship integrated between man/machine (human/nonhuman), in a non-binary, non-opposed, and non-hierarchical nature.[73] In fact, in *societies of metadata*, the activity of learning from machines produces a synchronic, continuous, and

[69] Cf. Wroblewski (1988), p. 19.

[70] "Here is our broad characterisation of the concept of an 'area' of law: (1) a subset of the legal norms in the system; (2) which is intersubjectively recognised by the legal complex in that system as a subset of such norms" (Khaitan and Steel 2023, p. 78).

[71] Cf. Colas-Blaise and Dondero (2020), p. 11.

[72] Cf. Dondero et al. (2024), pp. 1–24.

[73] "Le postdualisme pense l'humain comme articulé à ce qui n'est pas lui, et non plus dans une position exceptionnelle ou dominante au sein de l'univers (Paveau 2012c)." (Paveau 2015, p. 02).

dynamic update, which makes the task of machine mimicry of languages and human gestures possible, which incorporates and reworks them.[74] In this way, the question is no longer implausible, and today's *Science* is already being produced with the use of *algorithms* for scientific research, which makes use of the data shared by the accumulation of scientific publications available and traceable on the *Web*. In fact, the growth of scientific information, the number of publications and scientific databases open and digitally available for consultation has shown vertiginous growth in recent decades.[75]

Automatic enunciation is a form of *machine-made-enunciation*, mediated by technological apparatus, generated from *algorithms*—given that they are systematically trained to carry out automatic operations—,[76] which have become skillful in imitating human abilities. There is a mediation by *computer languages* (*formal programming languages*), which are responsible for the programming of *general rules* through which the *process of enunciation* can carry out new *acts of enunciation*.[77] In fact, *programming language* is a *collective* and *hybrid actant*, which allows a combinatory of signs to carry out programmed operations.[78] Particularly, when it comes to *generative AI* operations, it is about thinking of *automatic enunciation* carrying out an *act of language* from *databases*.[79] A *database* is more than simply an *archive*, since it can be defined more technically and precisely as an *archive of archives*.[80] In this sense, the quality of *databases* is key for obtaining good results in processing information.[81]

The digital age has unlocked access to information and has been representing a true *cognitive revolution*.[82] In fact, the astounding advances in technoscience (TS), artificial intelligence (AI), from information applied to scientific research and robotics have started to open up a new horizon of understanding in the area of the *Science of Law*. This is because, in the *Sciences* in general, the question that has already arisen in our time is that concerning scientific production based on a *learning process*. This has implied a hybridization of the stages of scientific research and scien-

---

[74] "Le modèle de la cybernétique qui inaugure la société des métadonnées met en valeur une imbrication totale entre nos gestes quotidiens et les réponses de la machine algorithmique, 409 une sorte de modulation continuelle et réciproque entre les compétences inscrites dans les gestes corporels et l'incorporation de ces gestes par la machine algorithmique" (Dondero 2017, p. 409).

[75] *Vide* Bornmann and Mutz (2015), pp. 2215–2222.

[76] Cf. D'Armenio et al. (2024), para 27–29.

[77] Cf. Dondero et al. (2024), pp. 4–5.

[78] "Nous passons donc de l'enquête sur le concept d'actant collectif hybride homme-machine à celui d'énonciation, en considérant le langage de programmation comme un actant collectif à son tour hybride, car le langage naturel doit s'ajuster au référent machine, à savoir un système mécanisé qui fonctionne comme une combinatoire de signes (un et zéro)" (Dondero 2017, p. 410).

[79] Cf. Dondero et al. (2024), p. 3.

[80] "First of all, a database is not simply a collection of archives, but an archive of archives: it integrates the first two meanings—archives as heritage collections and digital resources" (D'Armenio et al. 2024, para 18).

[81] Cf. Dondero et al. (2024), p. 10.

[82] See Taylor (2017), pp. 01–02.

tific reasoning, in a relationship of accentuated proximity between *man–machine*. We think about the formation of a true techno-scientific frontier, in which the very production of knowledge is exclusively established on the basis of integrated robotic activities, the clearest realization of a *science 4.0*. From the unrealism in which this has already been imagined, to the current picture of *Science* produced with the use of *ChatGPT*, one can quickly move to the level of autonomized scientific production carried out exclusively by machines. The question of a *science without men*, cybernetically mediated, occupies the scene, leaving the idea that scientific activity implies a *human act* by excellence in the past. A *science without a human face* is beginning to emerge.

6.2 *Jurist-Prometheus: A Model of a Post-humanist Jurist*

In his work *Law's empire* (1986), Ronald Dworkin invented the *judge-Hercules* model, to deal with complex decision-making tasks of judges. *Judge-Hercules* is an ideal projection of a judge (*judge-imaginary*),[83] which is characterized by its high *moral qualities*, endowed with a superhuman talent, namely, sagacity, wisdom, and infinite time.[84] The criticism made by Jürgen Habermas about the overload in the area of the personality of *judge-Hercules*, endowed with hyperbolic virtues, points to the idea that it should be freed from the *solipsism* of a task carried out in an individual and monological way,[85] in order to gamble on another version, that of unloading cognitive demands that fall on the judge in the dimension of the *procedure*.[86]

Currently, this debate can be taken up again, to be contextualized in another environment. This is because the question is reignited, in the face of the advances in technology, to the extent that the *cognitive revolution* opens up new perspectives to the question of access to knowledge. Thus, this philosophical debate, which has been aligned with a group of questions around the dispute over *reason*, should be *resituated*, in face of the new challenges of historical time, especially in times when lines of post-humanist thinking are emerging, from which it has become possible to postulate the end of humanism and the empire of machines.[87] However, it must be projected not from the perspective of the activity of jurisdiction, but from the perspective of the activity of producing legal knowledge, to the extent that this carries out the task of offering a qualified *pre-view* and assisting in the process of solving social conflicts.

[83] Cf. Dworkin (2014), p. 287.

[84] Cf. Dworkin (2014), p. 294.

[85] Cf. Habermas (2003), p. 277.

[86] Cf. Habermas (2003), p. 278.

[87] "El posthumanismo implica la versión «fuerte» de esas proyecciones tecnocientíficas al ámbito de lo humano y, desde sus enfoques, no se duda en postular la sustitución del paradigma humanista por el paradigma posthumanista" (Pérez Luño 2021, p. 273).

In this line of work, which involves *scientific imagination*, I would like to propose the model of the *jurist-Prometheus*, to deal with epistemic complex tasks of the *General Theory of Law*, in the digital age. The figure of Prometheus is taken from Greek mythology, pointing to the Titan who has robbed the fire from the Gods, bringing it to men, making this *symbol of knowledge* something liberating for *humanity*. Precisely for this reason, the figure of the *jurist-Prometheus* would be responsible for liberating jurists of the digital age from a huge overload of work that implies the processing of data, information, extensive research on databases, consulting thousands of cases judged by Courts, as well as general knowledge, but especially in regard to questions concerning the universe of social conflicts and questions of justice. Since legal knowledge is not just any type of knowledge, but a form of knowledge crucial for promoting justice, for the pacification, equating, and balancing of society, so that the possession of fire would imply a *complete emancipation* of society from the imbalances that are congenital to it, for which jurists have endeavored to find solutions and ways of resolving conflicts.

Although he is not a real jurist, the *jurist-Prometheus* is endowed with infinite *cognitive capacity*—and, for this reason, he does not perform the rhetorical tasks of Hercules,[88] but the cognitive tasks of scientific reasoning of the *jurist-Prometheus*—, which makes him able to wisely equate any social conflict that comes to his attention, allowing the *General Theory of Law* to be the exercise of a form of knowledge on which society as a whole can safely and effectively rely. At a time when we are talking about *data justice*,[89] the advent of the *jurist-Prometheus* would be able to bring a figure of greater *cognitive capacity* to the area of Law—derived from the extremely high technological and algorithmic capacity with which it would be endowed—, in other words, with a *cognitive capacity* superior to established traditional legal knowledge[90] and, therefore, better able to respond to the challenges of the *General Theory of Law* of the digital age and advanced technology, by being endowed with infinite memory, speed of access to an unlimited stock of data, by being endowed with the ability to dedicate itself full-time to its cognitive operations.

With these high *technical qualities*, the *jurist-Prometheus* would be better able to: (1) respond to the high accumulation of information; (2) be aware of legislative changes in a context of a high degree of substitutability of normative texts; (3) meet the high level of complexity of present times; (4) meet the urgency of the demand for updating legal knowledge; (5) adapt to growing cognitive demands; (6) accumulate knowledge, in the form of an archive of data, in an unrestricted and unlimited way. The advantages that result from the activity of the *jurist-Prometheus* would be in its unlimited capacity for learning (*omniscience*), in its permanence beyond human finitude (*eternity*), in its increased capacity to gather data from diverse

---

[88] Cf. Witteveen (1990), pp. 227–254.

[89] Cf. Taylor (2017), p. 06.

[90] "Acorde con la célebre ley del método dialéctico que postula el paso de la cantidad a la calidad, la actitud posthumanista no duda en afirmar que nos hallamos ante un conocimiento cualitativamente distinto y superior al modus cognoscendi del pasado, gracias a las aportaciones de la IA" (Pérez Luño 2021, pp. 295–296).

matrices (*jurisprudence*, *science*, *legislation*), in the speed of processing data with obtaining answers, and the accuracy of the results obtained in real time (*omnipotence*), otherwise it would not have the proper characteristics of a *post-humanist jurist*.[91] It would be the stereotype of the *jurist-machine*, a typical post-human manifestation of work carried out by the community of jurists.

7 Algorithmic Rationality and the Reflexive Force of the *General Theory of Law*

7.1 Algorithmic Rationality and the Dehumanization of the Science of Law

From Jürgen Habermas's essay, *Technik und Wissenchaft als Ideologie* (1968), it is possible to understand the dynamics imposed by the innovative and disruptive nature of new technology. This is because *algorithmic rationality*, as a manifestation of *technoscientific rationality*, expels the world of life, the mediation of everyday language, social participation, and dimension of ethical values from its universe.[92] It turns the human-protagonist into a memorial figure of its programmed structure, since this universe is born in the image and likeness of human practices that are now mechanically optimized, in order to overcome its limits. From being a cog that holds *information* and *data*, by the centralizing logic of *Big Data*[93] the machine that takes care of some imitative aspects of *humanity* displaces the *human* in place, to situate him in his new universe, which is the place of *homo fabricatus*.[94]

His autonomy has been stripped away, and, now, the machine has taken his place, telling him what to do. There is in this a consummation of portions of existence that, gradually, also means a possession of portions of cognitive activities. The position of creator is abandoned by *homo fabricatus*, which now only becomes an *object* of robotic operations, begins to act conditioned by *technoscientific logic*, which functions as an ideological apparatus of highly developed societies.[95] Now, it is the transfer of *decision-making power* to the *operational system* that makes it the new holder of capacities and abilities for which machines were trained, expanding their ability to learn and imitate operations, previously considered exclusively human.

---

[91] "La dimensión ontológica del poshumanismo concibe un futuro de seres posthumanos omniscientes, omnipotentes y eternos" (Pérez Luño 2021, p. 300).

[92] Cf. Habermas (2001), p. 82.

[93] "If we think of today's computer society, underpinned by the 'big data' paradigm, the role of databases occupies a central place" (D'Armenio et al. 2024, para 17).

[94] Cf. Habermas (2001), p. 75.

[95] Cf. Habermas (2001), p. 74.

The question that now arises is precisely that, in the future, in a projective nature, the *General Theory of Law* will not be a product of human activity, but the result of robotically mediated activity, an activity that expresses an *algorithmic rationality*. Will legal thinking of the future be a thinking marked by generative artificial intelligence? Can jurists' *legal reasoning* be reduced to a mere collection of data? Will *algorithmic reasoning* become the new standard for legal reasoning. Anyway, the challenge is on for the community of jurists. We are trying to build a *science without scientists*, which is the equivalent to saying a *jurisprudence without jurists*. The ideal of the methodical and technical purification of the *Science of Law*, would now be meta-modeled by an idea of *Natural Science* taken to its maximum potential, restoring a *methodological tendency* that aims to find the *elementary mold* for configuring practices and knowledge specific to this area outside of the *Human and Social Sciences*. That is how a *new scientific mythology* is in the air, which is, by producing a science so impartial, so precise, so technical, so exact, so complete, that no scientist would be capable of the same.

7.2 General Theory of Law: Humanism, Self-understanding, and Social Criticism

In order to respond to this challenge, it is necessary to take a stand. And this is only possible on the basis of a particular theoretical perspective. And, given the current multiple tendencies in the field of the *General Theory of Law*—considering the huge range of schools and lines of analysis, among *jusnaturalists*, *juspositivists* (inclusivist and exclusivist), *realists*, *argumentatives*, *critics*, *Marxists*, and *non-positivists*—, this author has developed the *Theory of Realistic Humanism*,[96] a theoretical position that restores the link between *humanist reflection* and *legal reflection*. From this perspective of analysis, it is argued that the *rationality of Law* is not limited to a mere *technical rationality*—despite not completely dispensing of practical and operational exercise of this, as Eric Millard warns—,[97] implying a strong need for the criticism of reality, historically situated understanding, problematization of social coexistence, and elaboration of moral judgments about the complex combination of values.

The theoretical perspective of the *Theory of Realistic Humanism* avoids the excessively analytical stance—a characteristic that makes the *General Theory of Law* much less attractive, precisely because it dwells too much on the formal and abstract aspects—,[98] distancing itself from *theoretical isolationism* that is specific to the community of jurists, in order to develop a humanist, reflexive, critical, and

---

[96] Cf. Bittar (2024a, b).

[97] "La Théorie générale du Droit ne se substitue pas à un enseignement technique du droit positif. Elle doit au contraire le renforcer" (Millard 2006, p. 34).

[98] *Vide* Enoch (2015), p. 01.

situated approach. In this sense, the difference between the *Theory (Traditional General) of Law* (analytical, monodisciplinary, isolated, descriptive, positive norm, monological, neutral) and the *Theory (General Critical) of Law* (critical, interdisciplinary, emancipatory, democratic, dialogical, humanist) is at the exact point where the former envisages the knowledge of jurists as a *dissociative* and *exclusivist theoretical doing*, based on the purity of the method,[99] in regard to the relationship of the *Science of Law* with the *Humanities*, as the latter opts for the *associative* and *inclusive theoretical doing* by jurists,[100] in relation to the *Humanities*. The *Theory of Realistic Humanism* places the *General Theory of Law* at the "equidistant point" between the *universal consensuses* of the theorists of Law and the *realistic concreteness* of the local manifestations of empirical Positive Laws. It is from the intersecting of these two dimensions, it is possible to think about the formation of a *General Theory of Law* adequate for our times and adjusted to the local social challenges of each social reality regulated by the Positive Law of each community.

8 The Humanization of the *General Theory of Law*: An Understanding Based on the *Theory of Realistic Humanism*

8.1 General Theory of Law: Technification, Dehumanization, and Farewell to Reason

With this stance, developed in the field of the *General Theory of Law*, the *Theory of Realistic Humanism*—as a theoretical conception unfolded by the tradition of *Critical Theory* in a Latin-American context—,[101] takes a critical stance toward *post-humanist* theories. When *post-humanist* tendencies point to the definitive degradation of *humanity*, and its surpassing by the *machine*, there is a pointlessness in this that is inherent to every ideology.[102] It is the purpose of every *Critical Theory*, in the scope of the *General Theory of Law*, to formulate a criticism of *dehumanization*[103] that is contained in the project of the *desertification* of thinking. This is because the *Science* that is made up of only of crossing data, technically mediated, based on *algorithmic operations*, is the one that fully accomplishes the process of the *technification* of the scientific environment. *Scientific reason* would be tempted to say farewell to the tasks of *Science*, because now every *cognitive operation* would

[99] See Kelsen (2005), pp. 01–05.

[100] *Vide* Rodriguez (2010), p. 403.

[101] Cf. Bittar (2019), pp. 319–332.

[102] Cf. Habermas (2001), p. 74.

[103] "A tenor de ese designio se estaría produciendo, en el presente y en el inmediato futuro, un proceso de paulatina deshumanización de las sociedades y de la cultura, al que correlativamente serviría de fundamento legitimador una ideología suprahumanista" (Pérez Luño 2021, p. 304).

be established in the *realm of technique*. The criticism of *dehumanization* here signifies, also, the criticism of *technification* as a farewell to reflection. In the sense adopted by Pierluigi Basso Fossali, we can speak of a *criticism of computerized reason* (and of sensibility).[104] In contrast to *post-humanist* postures, the humanist and realistic vision presupposes not a farewell to reflection, as a typically human activity, but the most committed and profound entry into its universe. *Algorithmic rationality* is a reduction of the idea of *reason*, because it impoverishes (on the basis of a set of data) *prudential rationality* (experiential, axiological, historical, dialectical, and heuristic) that is specific to the area of Law.

The *Theory of Realistic Humanism* postulates the theoretical position according to which the reflexive quality and critique of the *General Theory of Law* depends on the expansion of the *view of the jurist*. The *view of the jurist* must shift from laws to focus on society, and, for this, the interdisciplinary exercise of meeting with the *Human and Social Sciences* is required. In short, the *General Theory of Law* partially fulfils its task, when it is only focused on the self-understanding of the legal system, approached formally and abstractly, in the way it has been conceived, by both Hans Kelsen, in his *Pure Theory of Law*,[105] and Norberto Bobbio, in his *Teoria dell'Ordinamento Giuridico*,[106] to the extent that they detached the relationship between *Law & Society*. Insofar as, in order to overcome this traditional way of conceiving the *object of study*, the *Theory of Realistic Humanism* proposes in the method of dialogue a situated understanding of *social reality* onto which systemized Law is projected, increasing the chances of reconnection between *Law & Society* and, also, the reconnection between *Law & Justice*.

8.2 General Theory of Law: Place of Discourse, Humanism, and Reflexive Force

The *Theory of Realistic Humanism* understands, therefore, that the *General Theory of Law* has a privileged *place of discourse*, situated in the *between worlds* of the *Human Sciences* and the *Science of Law*, playing the role of bringing between these cognitive universes closer together. With this, it becomes a *point of confluence* between the *Human and Social Sciences*—from which is draws the critical and analytical competence of social, historical, and cultural reality—and the *Normative Sciences of Law*—from which it draws specific, technical, and conceptual competence, from the internal universe of the operational problems of the legal system. Thus, it aims to articulate the internal perspective with the external perspective,

[104] Cf. Fossali (2024), para 19–27.

[105] "It is called a 'pure' theory of law, because it Only describes the law and attempts to eliminate from the object of this description everything that is not strictly law: Its aim is to free the Science of Law from alien elements" (Kelsen 2005, p. 01).

[106] *Vide* Bobbio (1999), p. 19.

producing a broadening of the *view of the jurist* about legal problems as sociohistorical–legal problems. The *General Theory of Law* works, in this way, as an aggregating theory by integrating knowledge, articulating cognitive spheres, allowing for the necessary porosity in the transit of content between the *Human and Social Sciences* and the *Normative Sciences of Law*,[107] to the extent in which it articulates the interest for the *reflexive function* and the *resolutive function*.

With this line of understanding, what is *human* in the *General Theory of Law* is that which cannot yet be sought in the mere *storage of data*. The *General Theory of Law* produced by machines would only be an expression of a *sterile*, *artificial*, *aseptic*, and *data-centered methodological* vision.[108] What there is in the *General Theory of Law* has to do with: (1) the exercise of human sensitivity; (2) emancipatory rationality; (3) the situated reflection in the face of historical challenges; (4) the differentiation of ideological nuances that define different approaches to the understanding of the universes of meaning; (5) the understanding of social, cultural, and contextual transformations; (6) the demands for hermeneutic positioning; (7) the alignment in the face of philosophical trends; (8) the ability to propose conditions for social transformation; (9) the vision through which modifications of techniques and traditional legal concepts are suggested; (10) the flexibility to change position and adapt to epochal demands.

Thus, jurists would be invited to interact with the products extracted from machines, now placing themselves at the service of *artificial intelligence* (AI). For a *Science of Law* that is quantitometric, numerized, and aimed toward a rationality of ends, all this *makes even more sense*. On the contrary, for a critical and situated *Science of Law*, this *makes even less sense*, considering the very *meaning* of what is understood by the specific activity of the *Science of Law*. The *force of reflection* (*reflexive knowledge*)—taken here as the manifestation of the ability to think critically about the relationship between man and man, as well as the relationship of man and the world—, it cannot be weakened, in favor of a type of *technical knowledge*.[109] Denouncing the technocratic nature of *algorithmic rationality* implies a concern for the restoration of *reflexive force*, a quality of *emancipatory reason* derived from the *Enlightenment*, and for the search of horizons of understanding that are capable of restoring the place of *fair* in the world of conflicts and disputes amongst rights.

To this extent, the demand for what the processes of producing legal knowledge should keep alive is the *human* task of *thinking about the challenges of coexistence*, inscribing them on a *horizon of emancipation*. *Emancipatory reason* should be capable of thinking about clearing the ways for the creation of *new rights*, and not reproducing the history of rights already conquered and assimilated. It is true that

[107] *Vide* Vesting (2015), pp. 42–43.

[108] "El riesgo que se deriva del método cognoscitivo del posthumanismo, reside, precisamente, en que no nos ofrece una visión de la realidad, sino que propone una realidad construida artificialmente, a través de la IA, el Big Data y los algoritmos diseñados para su elaboración" (Pérez Luño 2021, p. 300).

[109] Cf. Habermas (2001), p. 81.

scientific research can have stages carried out by an *algorithm*—whose instrumental task can function as an auxiliary and supporting element in the process of searching for and producing knowledge—, but this is provided that the last word is not the effective (and committed) manifestation of a *human gesture*. In this domain, as in many others, *moral sense* is not something that can be expected from machines, which reinforces the connection between *Law & Moral*, within the process of forming categories that should guide the genesis of the *discourse* of the *General Theory of Law*. In any case, given the current times, even if the *jurist-Prometheus* does come into existence—and, shortly, from speculation, this will become a fact, insofar as humanity is on the verge of this—, its activity will never be able to perform with the same acuity that only men are capable of achieving, except as an instrument or support for the exercise of human reflection.

9 Conclusions

The *General Theory of Law* is a field of work that is indispensable for the jurists' self-understanding about the way the legal system works. The *General Theory of Law* offers jurists a *theoretical–philosophical discourse* that analyzes and discusses how the operations of *legal discourse* within the legal system work. The semiotic approach makes a valuable contribution, when the topic is the understanding, one wants to have of how *legal discourses* work. It is in this way that the *General Theory of Law* has been brought into focus, in order to emphasize its specificity, as a manifestation of a *metalanguage* that works within *legal discourses*.

The *General Theory of Law* is currently going through a state of *crisis of meaning*, which is why it has lost its representativeness in the *interdiscursive* relationship with other *Normative Sciences of Law*. Not being able to focus only on conceptual achievements from the past, the discipline must move forward and be updated, in order to fully perform its reflexive task. This implies the task of overcoming the *desynchronization* between the *reflexive function* of the *General Theory of Law* and the *resolutive function* of the *Normative Sciences of Law*, so that the latter does not become the *vanguard*, as the former becomes a *pale background* for the theoretical interests of jurists.

Nowadays, the *Normative Sciences of Law* have gone through a phase of development of high *fragmentation*, a phenomenon that provokes the loss of the *general vision* of the unity of the legal system. In view of this, one of the effects has been the emergence of the *General Theories of Specialities*, which introduce a *reflexive function* in fields traditionally marked by the *resolutive function*. But, the *General Theories of Specialities* are unable to subsume the role of the *General Theory of Law*, as they are not sufficiently extensive. The latter maintains a *federative* relationship with the former, by conforming them on the basis of the *cognitive unity* of the legal system. From its *discursive place*, it takes a *cyclopean view* on the multiplicity of the disciplines of Law, as the *Normative Sciences of Law* take a *specialized view*. It forms, therefore, a *diegetic* and *constituent discourse*, of paramount importance for the self-understanding of Law.

The *General Theory of Law* formulates *theoretical enunciations* aimed at describing the way the legal system works, playing a *nomological* role, offering an integrated vision on the diversity of legal phenomena studied. This allows us to understand that it is achieved, like all *Science*, through the activities of *scientific enunciation*—as a cognitive producer of methodological and rational knowledge, validated by the scientific community—, given that it is from this that *scientific discourse* emerges, which is dedicated to achieving the *effect of meaning of objectivity* (completeness and veracity) and the *persuasive doing* (persuasion and convincing) directed at the scientific community. In short, the *scientific enunciations* that are specific to the *General Theory of Law* are endowed with specific qualities, which are analyzed throughout the study, with views to highlight their more specific characteristics (universal, abstract, empirical–analytical, theoretical, rational and demonstrable, complex, unifying, general, polemic, argumentative). The *General Theory of Law* forms, therefore, a *metascientific discourse*, of importance for the *Science of Law*, as it carries out the task of *legal–scientific language* that analyzes the normative phenomena specific to Law. The *metalanguage* specific to the *General Theory of Law* is marked by the *quadruple isotopy* (fourth-level metalanguage in relation to the referent world), dealing with the concept of Law. In turn, the *Philosophy of Law* is marked by the *quintuple isotopy*, dealing with the concept of justice. While the *General Theory of Law* deals with legal *macro-meaning*, the *Normative Sciences of Law* deal with the specialized *micro-meaning* of Law.

Finally, with technological innovations, *automatic enunciation* has made the construction of *Science* by machines possible, by using *algorithms* for scientific research. *Programming language* forms a *collective and hybrid actant* that performs acts based on *databases*. It is in this environment that the creation of an *ideal figure* is projected, that of *jurist-Prometheus*, a jurist who deals with the *General Theory of Law*, being endowed with a high cognitive ability, processing information with infinite memory, from an unlimited stock of data. The *jurist-Prometheus* would be further ahead in his ability to respond to the challenges of the emergency of *algorithmic rationality*. In this sense, the greater the techno-scientific advance, *algorithmic rationality* will increasingly occupy more space in legal reasoning in the process of shaping the *General Theory of Law* of the digital age.

The criticism of this new *scientific mythology* can be made from the line of analysis of the *Theory of Realistic Humanism*, which argues that the rationality of Law is not limited to a *technical rationality*. As for *Critical Theory*, it formulates the criticism of *dehumanization* promoted by the advances of *post-humanist discourses*, whose task has been to promote an exaltation of the *realm of technique*. The criticism of *algorithmic rationality* points to the need to preserve *prudential rationality* in the field of Law. The privileged *place of discourse* of the *General Theory of Law*, as an *advanced post* of *legal knowledge*, cannot be delegated to machines, otherwise the loss of *reflexive* and *emancipatory force* of Law will be lost in the fight for renewed horizons of justice. This would be the equivalent to a *farewell to reason*, in a highly strategic field for a sensitive, problematic, morally committed, and socially relevant dimension of human knowledge, which is the *Science of Law*.

References

Abboud G, Carnio HG, Oliveira RT (2015) Introdução à Teoria e Filosofia do Direito, 3rd edn. Revista dos Tribunais, São Paulo

Almeida FDM (2015) Formação da Teoria do Direito Administrativo no Brasil. Quartier Latin, São Paulo

Barzotto LF (2017) Teoria do Direito. Livraria do Advogado, Porto Alegre

Beividas W (2019) Une épistémologie discursive en construction. In: Zinna A, Moreno LR (eds) Collection Études: L'imanence en jeu. CAMS/O, Toulouse, pp 85–101. Disponível em: https://mediationsemiotiques.com/. Acesso em 21.12.2024

Bergel J-L (2006) Teoria Geral do Direito (trans: Maria Ermantina de Almeida Prado Galvão). Martins Fontes, São Paulo

Bittar CA (2007) Teoria Geral do Direito Civil, 2nd edn. Forense Universitária, Rio de Janeiro

Bittar ECB (2019) A humanistic turn in critical legal theory: the birth of a new conception in Brazilian legal theory. In: Bittar ECB (ed) Philosophy of law: global dialogues, controversial issues and challenges of justice. Quartier Latin, São Paulo, pp 319–332

Bittar ECB (2022a) Linguagem jurídica: semiótica, discurso e direito, 8th edn. Saraiva, São Paulo

Bittar ECB (2022b) Semiotics of law, science of low and legal meaning: analysis of the status of legal dogmatics. Signata 13:93–116. https://journals.openedition.org/signata/4129

Bittar ECB (2023) Introduction. Remarques historiques sur la relation entre le Droit et le Langage. Actes Sémiotiques 128:01–25. https://www.unilim.fr/actes-semiotiques/7831&file=1/

Bittar ECB (2024a) Introdução ao estudo do Direito: humanismo, democracia e justiça, 4th edn. Saraiva, São Paulo

Bittar ECB (2024b) La machine du droit: le modèle de maillage du système juridique et les transformations du sens juridique. Actes Sémiotiques 130:159–178. https://www.unilim.fr/actes-semiotiques/8264

Blalock C (2014) Neoliberalism and the crisis of legal theory. Law Contemp Problems 77(4):71–103

Bobbio B (1999) Teoria do ordenamento jurídico (trans: Maria C. L. C. Santos), 10th edn. Editora Unb, Brasília

Bobbio B (2015) Estudos para uma Teoria Geral do Direito (trans: Daniela Beccaccia Versiani). Manole, São Paulo

Bornmann L, Mutz B (2015) Growth rates of modern science: a bibliometric analysis based on the number of publications and cited references. J Assoc Inf Sci Technol 66(11):2215–2222. https://asistdl.onlinelibrary.wiley.com/doi/pdfdirect/10.1002/asi.23329

Broekman JM, Backer LC (2013) Lawyers making meaning. Springer, New York

Camillo C (2019) Manual da Teoria Geral do Direito. Almedina, São Paulo

Castanheira Neves A (2003) A crise atual da Filosofia do Direito no contexto da crise global da Filosofia. Coimbra Editora, Coimbra

Catania A (2010) Manuale di Teoria Generale del Diritto. Laterza, Lecce

Colas-Blaise M, Dondero MG (2020) Présentation. Semen, 49. (online). https://doi.org/10.4000/semen.14233

Cossutta F (2020) Questions de méthode. Comment aborder la conceptualisation philosophique d'un point de vue discursif. In: Cossutta F (ed) Les concepts en philosophie. Limoges, Lambert Lucas, pp 15–39

D'Armenio E, Dilière A, Dondero MG (2024) Semiotics of Machinic co-enunciation; about generative models. Signata 15. (online). http://journals.openedition.org/signata/5290

Del Vecchio G (1979) Lições de Filosofia do Direito (trans: António José Brandão), 5th edn. Arménio Amado, Coimbra
Delmas-Marty M (2004) Por um direito comum. Translated by Maria Ermantina de Almeida Prado Galvão. Martins Fontes, São Paulo
Dickson J (2001) Legal theory today: evaluation and legal theory. Hart Publishing, Oxford
Dickson J (2017) Why general jurisprudence is interesting. Crítica: Revista Hispanoamericana de Filosofia 49(147):11–39
Dinamarco CR, Lopes BVC (2016) Teoria Geral do novo Processo Civil. Malheiros, São Paulo
Dondero MG (2017) Le travail des algorithmes: quelques réflexions sur l'actancialité et l'énonciation. In: Bertrand D, Bordron J-F, Darrault I, Fontanille J (eds) Greimas aujourd'hui: l'avenir de la structure. Actes du Congrès de l'Association Française de Sémiotique, AFS Éditions, pp 405–416
Dondero MG, Castro GHR, Schwartzmann MN (2024) Inteligência artificial e enunciação: análise de grandes coleções de imagens e geração automática via Midjourney. Todas as Letras—Revista de Língua e Literatura 26(2):1–24. https://doi.org/10.5935/1980-6914/eLETTR17164
Dupoux E (2018) Cognitive science in the era of artificial intelligence. Cognition 173:43–59. https://www.sciencedirect.com/science/article/abs/pii/S0010027717303013
Dworkin R (2014) O império do Direito. Trad. Jeferson Luiz Camargo, 3rd edn. Martins Fontes, São Paulo
Eal E (2004) Langue du droit et doctrine: la linguistique juridique au servisse de l'accessiblité internationalisée des contributions doctrinales. Revue Générale de Droit 34(02):233–265. Disponible sur: https://id.erudit.org/iderudit/1027252ar. Accès en 17.06.2025
Enoch D (2015) Is general jurisprudence interesting?. SSRN(1) (online). https://ssrn.com/abstract=2601537 or https://doi.org/10.2139/ssrn.2601537
Finnis J (2011) Natural law and natural rights, 2nd edn. Oxford University Press, New York
Finnis J (2021) What is the philosophy of law? Rivista di Filosofia del Diritto 1:67–78
Fiorin JL (2016) As astúcias da enunciação. São Paulo: Contexto
Fossali PB (2024) Les images entre formes symboliques et humanités numériques: une introduction. Signata 14:online. http://journals.openedition.org/signata/4964
Gardner J (2001) Legal positivism: 51/2 myths. Am J Jurisprudence 46:01–40
Gomes MGM (2012) Bases para uma Teoria Geral da Parte Especial do Direito Penal. USP, Tese de Livre Docência, São Paulo
Goodrich P (1984a) Legal discourse: studies in linguistics, rhetoric and legal analysis. University of Edinburgh, Edinburgh
Goodrich P (1984b) Law and language: na historical and critical introduction. J Law Soc 11:173–206. https://larc.cardozo.yu.edu/faculty-articles/333
Greimas AJ (1974) L'énonciation: une posture épistémologique. Significação: Revista de Cultura Audiovisual 01:9–25
Greimas AJ (1976a) Sémiotique et Sciences Sociales. Seuil, Paris
Greimas AJ (1976b) Semiótica do discurso científico: da modalidade (trans: Cidmar Teodoro Pais). Difel, São Paulo
Greimas AJ, Courtés J (1993) Sémiotique: disctionnaire raisonné de théorie du langage. Hachette, Paris
Guastini R (2005) Das fontes às normas (trans: Edson Bini). Quartier Latin, São Paulo
Habermas J (2003) Direito e democracia: entre facticidade e validade, vol 1 e 2. Tempo Brasileiro, Rio de Janeiro
Habermas J (2005) Logique des Sciences Sociales. Traduit par Rainer Rochlitz. Presses Universitaires de France, Paris
Habermas J (2021) Técnica e ciência como ideologia (trans: Artur Morão). Edições 70, Lisboa
Hart HLA (1986) O conceito de Direito. Translated by a. Ribeiro Mendes. Fundação Calouste Gulbenkian, Lisboa
Jackson BS (1985) Semiotics and legal theory. Routledge & Paul Kegan, London

Karl L (1989) Metodologia da ciência do Direito (trans: José Lamego), 2nd edn. Fundação Calouste Gulbenkian, Lisboa

Kaufmann A (2002) Filosofía del derecho. Traducción de Luis Villar Borda y Ana María Montoya. Universidad Externado de Colombia, Bogotá

Kaufmann A, Hassemer W (2002) Introdução à Filosofia do Direito e à Teoria do Direito contemporâneas (trans: Marcos Keel e Manuel Seca de Oliveira). Fundação Calouste Gulbenkian, Lisboa

Kelsen H (1976) Teoria Pura do Direito (trans: João Baptista Machado), 4th edn. Arménio Amado, Coimbra

Kelsen H (2000) Teoria Geral do Direito e do Estado (trans: Luís Carlos Borges). Martins Fontes, São Paulo

Kelsen H (2005) Pure theory of law (trans: max knight). The Law Book Exchange, New Jersey

Khaitan T, Steel S (2023) Areas of law: the questions in special jurisprudence. Oxf J Leg Stud 43(01):76–96. https://doi.org/10.1093/ojls/gqac025

Kuhn TS (2003) A estrutura das revoluções científicas (trans: Beatriz Vianna Boeira and Nelson Boeira), 7th edn. Perspectiva, São Paulo

Luhmann N (2005) A realidade dos meios de comunicação (trans: Ciro Marcondes Filho). Paulus, São Paulo

Machado JB (2014) Introdução ao direito e ao discurso legitimador. 22ª. reimpressão. Almedina, Coimbra

Maingueneau D (2008a) Gênese dos discursos (trans: Sírio Possenti). Parábola, São Paulo

Maingueneau D (2008b) Cenas da enunciação (trans: Sírio Possenti e Maria Cecilia Pérez de Souza e Silva). Parábola, São Paulo

Maingueneau D (2020) Cartographie philosophique et extraction de concepts. In: Cossutta F (ed) Les concepts en philosophie. Lambert Lucas, Limoges, pp 201–217

Marmor A (2006) Legal positivism: still descriptive and morally neutral. Oxf J Leg Stud 26(4):683–704

Marmor A, Sarch A (2019) The nature of law. The Stanford Encyclopedia of philosophy, metaphysics research lab. Stanford University (Online). https://plato.stanford.edu/archives/fall2019/entries/lawphil-nature/

Millard É (2006) Théorie Générale du Droit. Dalloz, Paris

Moor P (2010) Dynamique du système juridique: une théorie générale du Droit. Génève, Schulthess. Bruylant, Bruxelles

Neves AC (2003) A crise actual da Filosofia do Direito no contexto da crise global da Filosofia. Coimbra Editora, Coimbra

Ost F (2004) Raconter la loi: aux sources de l'imaginaire juridique. Odile Jacob, Paris

Ost F (2012) Quale filosofia del diritto? Rivista di Filosofia del Diritto 1:23–40. https://www.rivisteweb.it/doi/10.4477/37391

Ost F (2017) Para que sirve el derecho? Doxa: Cuadernos de Filosofía del Derecho 40:15–48. https://doxa.ua.es/issue/view/2017-n40

Ost F, Kerchov MV (2002) De la pyramide au réseau? Pour une théorie dialectique du droit. Publications des Facultés Universitaires Saint-Louis, Bruxelles

Paveau M-N (2015) Ce qui s'écrit dans les univers numériques. Itinéraires 01:online. journals.openedition.org/itineraires/2313

Pérez Luño AE (2021) El posthumanismo no es un humanismo. Doxa Cuadernos de Filosofía del Derecho 44:291–312. 10.14198/

Popper K (2000) Conjectures and refutations. Routledge and Keagan Paul, London, pp 33–39. 1963, from Theodore Schick, ed., Readings in the Philosophy of Science, Mayfield Publishing Company, Mountain View, CA pp. 9-13. https://www.kokdemir.info/courses/psk515/docs/KarlPopper.pdf

Raz J (1979) The authority of law: essays on law and morality. Oxford University Press, Oxford

Raz J (2011) Between authority and interpretation: on the theory of law and practical reason. Oxford University Press, Oxford
Rodriguez MA (2010) Entre calar y no calar: decir lo justo. Doxa: Cuadernos de Filosofia del Derecho 33:399–408
Romano S (2008) O ordenamento jurídico (trans: Arno Dal Ri Júnior). Fundação Boiteux, Florianópolis
Sgarbi A (2013) Introdução à teoria do direito. Marcial Pons, São Paulo
Tamanaha AZ (2017) A realistic theory of law. Cambridge University Press, Cambridge
Taylor L (2017) What is data justice? The case for connecting digital rights and freedoms globally. Big Data and Society 7:01–14. https://journals.sagepub.com/doi/pdf/10.1177/2053951717736335
Twining W (2005) General Jurisprudence. Anales de la Cátedra Francisco Suárez 39:645–688
Vesting T (2015) Teoria do Direito: uma introdução (trans: Gercélia B. de O. Mendes). Saraiva, São Paulo
Wieacker F (1993) História do Direito Privado moderno, 2nd edn. Fundação Calouste Gulbenkian, Lisboa
Witteeveen WJ (1990) The rhetorical labours of Hercules. Int J Semiotics Law 3:227–254. https://link.springer.com/journal/11196/volumes-and-issues/3-3
Wroblewski J (1988) Les langages juridiques: une typologie. Droit et société 8:13–27

Eduardo C. B. Bittar Associate Professor, *Department of Philosophy and General Theory of Law*, Faculty of Law, University of São Paulo (Brazil—USP). He was President of the *National Human Rights Association* (ANDHEP, 2009–2010). He was second Vice-President of the *Brazilian Association of Philosophy of Law* (ABRAFI—IVR/Brazil, 2009–2016). He was a *Visiting Professor* at the *Università di Bologna* (2017), a *Visiting Professor* at the *Université Paris-Nanterre* (2018), a *Visiting Researcher* at the *Collège de France* (2019), a *Visiting Professor* at the *University of Coimbra* (2023–2024) and a *Visiting Researcher* at the *Université Paris Cité* (2024–2025). He is Member of the *Association for Semiotic Studies* (IASS/AIS, 2026). He is member of the *Association Française de Sémiotique* (AFS, 2025). He is *Doctor Honoris Causa* of the *Universidade Federal do Mato Grosso* (UFMT). He is an 1-B Researcher at CNPq (2023–2026).

“New” Questions Concerning the Experience of the *Legal System* and the Problem of the Sources of Law or the *Place* and Claims of an *Internal Critical Approach*: Going Beyond the Possibilities of a *General Theory of Law*

Jose Manuel Aroso Linhares

Abstract This chapter explores the articulation between two of the major themes of Legal Theory that of the content of Law in its systemic intelligibility (the issue of the Legal System) and that of the constitution and manifestation of this same content in its effective practical social or practical-communitarian assimilation (the issue of the Sources of Law), treating this articulation (of assumed connections and presumed differences) as if it were at stake the counterpoint between two diverse territories.

The consideration of the origin or the emergence of this relatively unusual treatment “forces” us, in the first stage, to return to the remarkable (but no less difficult) convergence between *normativism and historicism* between the universal intelligibility of the norm-ratio and the plural theory of sources, involving Savigny’s legacy concerning the three *Rechstarten (Gewohnheitsrecht, Gesetzesrecht, Juristenrecht)* which we see constitutively assumed and reflexively thematized (even though differently) by *Scientific Conceptual Positivism and Allgemeine Rechtslehre.*

The second stage is, however, indispensable. It is now the opportunity to explore (in just one of its dimensions) the Hart/ Dworkin’s debate (and this also as a legacy assimilated by other fronts of the confrontation between *conventionalist positivism and non-positivism*). The dimension in question is precisely the one that, concerning Legal Theory, contrasts an *external moderate cognitive* approach and an *internal normative* one, but now, as it would be expected, dominantly focused on the discussion concerning the determination of the content of law and the *thesis of the social sources*: as if the tensions attributable to conventionalism (correlative to those that nineteenth century’s *Naturhistorische Methode* preserved) were precisely those

J. M. A. Linhares (✉)
University of Coimbra, Coimbra, Portugal

Univ Coimbra, UCILeR (University of Coimbra Institute for Legal Research), Faculty of Law, Coimbra, Portugal
e-mail: linhares@fd.uc.pt

E. C. B. Bittar (ed.), *General Theory of Law*,
https://doi.org/10.1007/978-3-032-22517-7_3

that relate the concept of *rule* (and its plausible *uses of general classificatory words*) with the infinite possibilities of the social sources illuminated by the *rule of recognition* (and its customary "nature").

From this discussion emerges the third stage, in which (*with* Dworkin, but above all beyond and even *versus* Dworkin) it is argued that our current situation, without prejudice to the benefits of external (certainly *analytically moderate*, but also *empirical-explicatively radical* and even *critically "alienated" external*) approaches, benefits from exposing Legal Theory to the possibilities of an *internal perspective* capable of paying attention to the multidimensionality of the Legal System and the plurality of (institutionalized or quasi-institutionalized) Legal Sources while considering the mapping of contemporary Legal Thinking from the perspective of a conception of Law which treats it (or its Western conformation) as a *form of life*, as a *project* and as a *tradition*.

1 Introduction

1.1 Beyond the Possibilities of a General Theory of Law

Should we go beyond the possibilities of a *General Theory of Law*? I begin by clarifying the purpose of this subtitle and the challenges to which its interrogative mode exposes us. The problem lies certainly less in the *formulation* itself and in the signifiers that compose it—or in the integrity of these signifiers, involving a claim of universality–generality and a theoretical rational (subject/object) structure (*General Theory* of Law)—than in the adequacy of this formulation (and these signifiers) to what, at the level of the perspective-*visée* and its thematic "objects," we now reasonably expect from a *certain* meta-dogmatic autonomous level of reflection *on*, *about*, or *regarding* Law (distinct from other meta-dogmatic levels, such as those that the field-horizon of *Philosophy of Law* and the specific domain of *Legal Methodology* effectively assume).

The issue is, however, more complex than it seems, oscillating between *on the one hand* what appears to be the absence of a problem and *on the other hand* what emerges as a context of *undecidability* (signaling the difficulty, if not impossibility, of an answer). Why the absence of a problem? Because we do not need a deconstructive way of thinking to recognize that a *signifier*, even the most accomplished or consecrated one, survives frequently the discursive contexts and social–institutional situations that generated it, gaining unexpected meanings with this openness (if not *instability*). Why a context of *undecidability*? Because the discussion about the plausibility of the *signifiers* (their felicitous or infelicitous survival, their determinability or indeterminability, their significant enrichment or impoverishment) is not likely to be pursued outside of a practical–cultural contextualization.[1]

[1] It is important to recall that, as far as Derrida's idiom is concerned, *undecidability* does not identify some "vague indeterminacy": it is always, on the contrary, "a *determinate* oscillation between

Does our current context allow us to persist in the globalizing (homogenizing) intelligibility of the claim to *generality* (*General* Theory of Law)? Should this claim identify the entire territory in question (giving specific meaning to this meta-dogmatic approach) or should it highlight just one of its trends (the one that assimilates a *certain* legacy)? And what about the signifier *Theory*? How far can this signifier be expected to go in this exercise of indefinite opening? What network of differences, if not *différances* (concerning the *signified*), does it allow? Are there criteria that can be (trans-contextually) built (conceived of), thus allowing a distinction between plausible and non-plausible assimilations? Does it make sense to admit (even though contextually) this aspiration to trans-contextuality? Last but not least, is it justifiable to ask these questions within a specific context, while being simultaneously aware that they remain trans-contextually unanswerable?

It is unequivocally recognizable *today* that *legal discourse* has experienced, in most part of the nineteenth century, an incandescent *time of theory* and that this theory was paradigmatically (or at least dominantly) assumed (autonomized) as *General* Legal *Theory*. A closer look allows us to realize, however, that this paradigmatic domain, as far as the meaning of the *dogmatic/ meta-dogmatic*, *scientific/ meta-scientific* relations is concerned, does not correspond to full unanimity. There is certainly the path pursued by the Anglo-American *non-formalist* positivism, in which the *claim to generality* (as a "description" of "what law is" that "is not tied to any particular legal system or legal culture")[2] remains inseparable from the project of an *analytical Jurisprudence*—and thus also inseparable from Austin's legacy (and the *external* exercise of demarcation of the *Province of Jurisprudence*), even when (significantly later) this analytical trend ends up overcoming the *command theory* ("the conception of law as the sovereign's coercive orders") in order to defend a new beginning ("a fresh start"), and, with it, a certain *moderate external point of view*—,[3] an overcoming that will make us arrive to the core themes of the Concept and Nature of Law and their *all-or-nothing* determination, respectively, assumed by Hart and Raz.[4]

There is, however, mainly the exploration of universality as *generality* in an explicit *normativistic* vein—stimulated by the possibilities of an *internal theoretical visée ([als] Erkenntnis des Rechtlichen aus rein Rechtlichen)*—,[5] which, in the

possibilities," which in turn "are themselves highly *determined* in strictly *defined* situations," i.e., "*pragmatically* determined" (Derrida 1988, p. 148).

[2] This is a well-known passage from Hart's Postscript and his dialogue with Dworkin (Hart 1994, pp. 239–240).

[3] Cf. Hart (1994), pp. 51, 56–58, 79–80, 88–90.

[4] According to Raz (2009), here clearly departing from Hart's preferred meaning, the claim about the *concept* of law is a parochial contingent one, the claim about the *nature* of law is in contrast an "universal" one, respecting "all law," and "all legal systems," and the identity of "adjudication, legislation, and legal reasoning, wherever they may be, and wherever they might be" (Raz 2009, p. 91).

[5] The words are by Roland Dubischar (1983, p. 24) (*Das Programm der dogmatische-positivistischen Rechtstheorie: Erkenntnis des Rechtlichen aus rein Rechtlichen*).

last quarter of the nineteenth century, was developed by the continental legal thinking (also with a projection in Langdellian American formalism): it is in fact this understanding of *generality* (inseparable from the Historical School's legacy) that is particularly relevant when we consider the formulation of *general theory* or *general doctrine*, since more than the independence regarding a specific (particular) legal order or culture (or more than this independence as a component of a descriptive–interpretative science *encore à faire*), what is at stake here, with an explicit demarcation from Austin's tentative (*Die Engländer (…) brechen überall die Fragestellung zu früh ab*),[6] is the intention to build (to make autonomous) a meta-dogmatic or trans-dogmatic theoretical approach (*[die] uns im Gründe überhaupt nicht Praktisches [lehrt]*)[7] and this one, while facing "ultimate how- and why-questions" concerning the claims to validity, legitimacy, and realizability of the *jus positum* (*als Begreifen des Wie und Warum des Rechts dieser Menschenwelt*)[8] in a decisive dialogue with (or as a constitutive piece of) a new *positivistische Rechstphilosophie*.

This means in fact presupposing that the process of self-rationalization of dogmatics (as a *dogmatic Science of Law* or *Science of Law* in its strict sense) is being successfully pursued (when not fundamentally concluded), which opens the door to a *nicht dogmatisches Rechtswissenschaft*, if not directly to a *philosophische (formelle) Rechtslehre*, which will then be theoretically free to experience (as its core-object) the relationship between juridicity, scientificity, and Method, while clarifying–constructing the universal conception of law that makes this relationship a successful one. I am obviously referring to the project of the so-called *Allgemeine Rechtstheorie*, *Rechtslehre*, or *Pronzipienlehre* (Merkel, Bergbohm, Bierling), whose contribution has been already recalled (*supra*, chap. "The Historical Genesis of the *(General) Theory of Law*, and Beyond: Origins, Autonomy, and Methods"), without however forgetting that the territory thus explored is more complex and diverse (as well as less closed and immune to external challenges) than it seems at first glance.[9]

And yet, if it seems entirely justified to associate most part of the nineteenth century and the dawn of the twentieth century with a time of *General* Legal *Theory*, is it plausible to preserve this last formulation to characterize the twilight of the twentieth century and the beginning of the twenty-first century?

Why shouldn't our time also be identified as an Age of *General* Legal *Theory*? The answer is quite clear. The paths opened by the nineteenth-century analytical general legal theory (whether considered from the perspective of *General Jurisprudence* or in light of the *Allgemeine Rechtslehre*) have not ceased to be followed. Quite the contrary, they have been enriched by new possibilities (opened by successive analytical readings of the *linguistic turn*) and have even recently (during the last four decades) received significant impetus—generated on the one hand by

[6] Bergbohm (1892–1973), p. 14.

[7] Bergbohm (1892–1973), p. 103.

[8] Bergbohm (1892–1973), p. 103.

[9] See in this sense the development that I propose *in* Linhares (2009), pp. 261–314.

the reinvention of foundational or conventional positivism, opposing exclusive and inclusive-incorporationist proposals (Raz, Waluchov, Shapiro, Marmor, Kramer, Coleman, Postema), and on the other by the flourishing of a certain *neue Rechtswissenschaftstheorie* (Auer, Lepsius, Somek, Vesting, Bumke), this one assuming the plurality of legal sciences and thus systematically thematizing the intradisciplinarity of academic legal thinking.

And yet, if these paths continue to be vibrantly frequented, the truth is that they have lost their dominant and exclusive position, appearing instead as possibilities among other possibilities (those that the discourse of the twentieth century made inevitable). Is this enough to renounce a stable (or even consecrated) *label*, thus challenging the institutional situations that prolong it? I would say it is. Adding that the clarifications that this renouncement provokes are at least interesting or productive.[10] Just as it is (at least) productive to recognize some *new* meanings of the signifier *Theory* (this one preserved as if *on the edge*). So that we are able to conclude that ours is simply another (no less powerful) time of legal *Theory* (with the signifier "*Theory*," certainly not by chance, written between quotation marks!): beyond the suppression of the qualifier *general*, it is in fact indispensable to pay attention to the expansion—beyond a strict *subject/object* epistemic structure—of this signifier....[11]

1.2 Expanding the Signifier Legal "Theory"

Two words should suffice here to allude to this process of expansion, presenting, as if in flashes, the main alternative *modes* (or *"manners"*) that, considering *Legal Theory*, the last hundred years have made available. I will outline those alternatives using (overlapping) two expository resources (among many possible ones): the counterpoint between *litige* and *différend* inspired by Lyotard's proposal (Lyotard

[10] Another productive exercise of renunciation (parallel to this one) is certainly that which sacrifices the category *general principles of law* (and prefers the term *normative principles*). Such renunciation, also questioning a strongly established practice, exposes in fact the insurmountable connection of these *general principles* to a certain conception (privileging the so-called *principles as ratio*), while also presupposing a counterpoint with two other conceptions (*principles as intentio* and *principles as jus*). While principles as *ratio* correspond to the normativistic *general principles of law* obtained through a logical operation of *concentration* (as a process of "quantitative simplification," if not as a discovery-*Auffindung* of a plausible logical *center*), principles as *intentio* correspond to an experience of the principles conceived of as pre-juridical moral or communitarian regulative intentions, which become constitutively binding only through authoritarian (statutory or judicial) decisions. To experience principles as jus is finally taking seriously (with all the methodological implications) that principles objectify specifically juridical contents and should be treated as autonomous *law in force* (benefitting from a presumption of validity). For a development of this counterpoint, exploring the different origins and legacies involved, *see* Linhares (2012b).

[11] While considering the reflective level in question (if not its distinctiveness concerning other meta-dogmatic arenas), the survival of the signifier theory is only plausible if we admit that, in our current circumstances, the epistemic axis represents also just one possibility among others.

1983, pp. 9, 16 and 202–209) and the distinction between *internal* and *external* points of view consecrated by Hart's analytical hermeneutics and reinterpreted by Postema (Hart 1994, pp. 88–89, Postema 2011, pp. 287–289). This combination allows us to simplify the available spectrum of possibilities into three major axes, which in turn offer authentic *front lines*.

1.2.1 The first *front de combat* is the one in which the opponents converge on the presupposition of a *subject/ object* (cognitive-theoretical) structural scheme and on a (more or less explicit) program of epistemological unity (justifying an *external point of view*)—if you will, on the global conception of a *Theory of Law* as *Science* (illuminated by the axis of *episteme* and the methodical procedures that it allows)—, diverging however (*le litige!*) on the representation of the relevant object (at one pole autonomizing normativity as an ensemble of norms or rules, at the other pole treating normativity as a component of empirically explainable regularities), as well as on the way in which, through this representation of the object, they experience the balance between *episteme* and *techné* and the possibility of a *theoretical pluralism* (Popper, Hans Albert), but also the intentions of the discourse (*analytical* versus *empirical*), as well as the configuration of the external point of view (*moderate* versus *radical* or *extreme*).[12]

Even without all these specifications, this dispute-*litige* was already underlying the various conflicts that, during the nineteenth century, pitted normativisms and other formalisms against command theories, utilitarianisms, and other teleological approaches (including the American expressions of pragmatic instrumentalism). At the explicit level of *Legal Theory*, however, its full explosion emerged at the dawn of the twentieth century, with the famous debate between Kelsen and Ehrlich. It can indeed be said that, with this debate, was thus stabilized the dispute, which, fueled by a succession of counterposed fires (going from *Neukantianismus* and *Logischer Positivismus* to *sociological jurisprudences* and *social engineering projects*), allows us even today to contrast the lines-veins of the (internal) *allgemeine Lehre* and of the (external) *Rechtstheorie* (*als Realwissenschaft und/oder technologische Jurisprudenz*), the first dealing with an immanent formal–structural (and

[12] The *moderate external point of view ("moderate" EPOV)* describes analytically the rules or the structures of language *from the outside* while giving full play to their internal dimensions and the normativity these involve—or rather, if we want, *acknowledging* but not *taking up* an *internal point of view* (*IPOV*) (Postema 2011, pp. 286–287). The "radical" or "extreme" EPOV—and the *theoretical cut* it introduces—treats normativity and linguistic facts as components of empirically explainable regularities:

> ["[W]e can if we choose to occupy the position of an observer who does not even refer in this way to the internal point of view of the group. Such an observer is content merely to record the regularities of observable behaviour (…). If, however, the observer really keeps austerely to this extreme external point of view and does not give any account of the manner in which members of the group who accept the rules view their own regular behaviour, his description of their life cannot be in terms of rules at all, and so not in the terms of the rule-dependent notions of obligation or duty. Instead, it will be in terms of observable regularities of conduct, predictions, probabilities, and signs…." (Hart 1994, p. 89)].

analytical–categorical) determination of legal normativity and its concept(s) (justifying an *external moderate point of view*), the second addressing law as *factum–object* (if not reality–behavior), thus empirically determinable, in its sociological, psychological, semiotic, probabilistic, systemic, or economic intelligibilities (developing an *external radical point of view*).

1.2.2 The second front allows the identification of perspectives that converge in the defense of a scientific discourse—i.e., in the conclusion-claim to configure relevant meta-normative reflection from the perspective of this discourse (and with the intentions and information basis it makes available)—, diverging however in the way they conceive of this discourse and the intentions–commitments that legitimize it (*"traditional"* theory versus *"critical"* theory)—but also and very especially in the meaning they attribute to a *rational* intervention. It is in the so-called *Positivismusstreit* (Dahm 1994) that we find the full emergence of this *litige* (from the very beginning denounced as a *faux litige*... and thus feeding the challenges and wounds of a *diférend*).

With one side of the barricade constituted by the cognitive–objectivist (analytical and empirical) approaches that we have identified above (and by the legacies that these have been assimilating, with all the new breaths allowed) [*supra*, Sect. 1.2.1.] ... and with the other side denouncing the *"traditional"* understanding of science that sustains such approaches (and their technologically conceived pragmatic conversions)—but then also submitting the province of *Legal Theory* (and this as *kritische Theorie*) to the "ethical impulse" of an open (*materialist*) *dialectics* and to the project of a self-overcoming transformation (if not "sublimation"-*Aufhebung*) of philosophy (which experiences it as a *concrete philosophy*) ... as well as to the possibilities–demands of a "commitment to participation" (which is also a promise of transformation–"emancipation" of praxis).[13]

1.2.3 The third front (a more complex one, certainly because internally more diversified) includes perspectives that converge on the urgency of an alternative to the two previous ones—i.e., on the need to detach the "theory" of law from its founding commitment to a claim of scientificity—, as well as on the conclusion-claim to reinvent Aristotelian phronesis—, diverging in turn on the way they understand this alternative: on the type of rational experience they make correspond to it, on the program they call for, on the intentions–objectives they impute to the leading perspective. Still simplifying, we can distinguish two major possible paths on this front (also as *litiges* convertible into *différends*).

1.2.3.1 On the one hand, there is a kind of a second-generation critical-philosophical discourse (assimilated by significantly different trends "within" *Critical Legal Studies* and *Postmodern Jurisprudences*), the construction of which, whilst resisting the metanarratives of totality opened up by Hegelian and Marxist discourses (if not directly by the possibilities of dialectic-materialist critical theories), reconciles with a *sui generis* return to Aristotle two major (surprisingly diverse) legacies, more or less selectively overlapped, attributable respectively to

[13] *See* the synthesis proposed by Buckel (2006), pp. 117–137.

Kant and Nietszche: it is as if this new critical attitude and the practical philosophy, if not anti-philosophy, it engenders ("*un questionnement sur les fondements [qui] n'est ni fondationaliste ni anti-fondationaliste*")[14] should develop itself *on the one hand* reinventing a contemporary genealogy of the practical worlds and their *continuum, on the other hand* inscribing (integrating) in this genealogy an autonomous (quasi transcendental) reconstitution of conditions of possibility/ impossibility.

The full articulation of these two main legacies is, in fact, decided in the interplay of three major contributions. The first derives from Foucault's *microphysics of power* (Foucault 1976, pp. 117–127)—and involves his archaeological and genealogical rewriting of *l'Âge de l'homme*, if not his *aesthetics of existence*—, the second assimilates Lyotard's disputes between *phrases* and *genres de discours*—as well as his *incommensurability theorem* (Welsch 1991, pp. 251–256) and his *experience of community as a promise* (Lyotard 1990, pp. 61–84)—, the third assumes Derrida's *programmatological interpretation* (Derrida 1988, p. 159, note 16) and the way in which this (as a specific *intersection of a pragmatics and a grammatology*) involves the *justice/deconstruction* connection, as well as a certain *economy of violence* (*une philosophie de la non-violence qui [choisit] la moindre violence*) (Derrida 1967, p. 136 note 1]. It is as if we were invoking the (reunited or separated) spells of a *political "morality"* (based on the Foucauldian experience of an immanent capillary network of *powers* and *resistances*), of an *aesthetics/anesthetics of the sublime* (justified through a Lyotardian reinvention of Kant's *reflexive judgment*), and a radically autonomous *ethics of alterity* (committed to the Derridean translation of Levinas' *infinite responsibility*)...

1.2.3.2 Concerning the return of *phronesis*, there is however another path (the first, moreover, to emerge historically). I refer, evidently, to the one that we may acknowledge by considering a certain *nonanalytical* "rehabilitation of practical philosophy" (Gadamer, Viehweg, Riedel, Bubner) [Riedel 1972–1974] and this one as a discourse of *constitutive immanence*, developing an internal perspective on *praxis* (and its foundational, regulative, and constitutive moments). This is, in fact, a discourse whose conditions only became possible in the second half of the twentieth century, while combining (overlapping) the modern acquisition of *intentional–cultural subjectivity* with a practical–existential experience of *historicity* (as a radical *constitutive historicity*)—the former making us responsible for the authorship-*inventio* of our practical worlds (their goals and values), the latter submitting this *invention* to indispensable self-reflexive differentiations concerning the factors and conditions, but also the different dynamics and varying degrees of vulnerability to contingence (with the possibility of introducing a constitutive dialectic equilibrium between *societas* and *communitas*).

In parallel with the deconstructive rewriting of *phronesis* (even though with different outcomes), this rehabilitation reinvents the equilibrium of Aristotelian *intellectual virtues* as a major experience of *plurality* (a paradigmatic consecration of plural rational types), while simultaneously exploring the autonomous possibilities

[14] Cf. Derrida (1994), p. 22.

of *phronesis*, for once freed from the prevalence or predominance (or even from the methodic priority) of theoretical claims: freed from the theoretical-speculative claims due to the premodern integrative horizon of *sophia* (and its institutionalization of the connection *telos/ethos*) or from the theoretical–philosophical domestication ("consummation") of dialectics due to Hegel's legacy (forcing dialectics to forget its provenience-*Herkunft* and to breach its constitutive bond with *topics*) (Bubner 1990, pp. 9, 79 and 88–96)... but also freed from the theoretical–scientific colonization corresponding to the hypertrophy of *episteme*... and its irreversible appropriation of *technê* (*Sachkundheit*)—a hypertrophy and an appropriation that Modernity consummated as (or converted into) *metaphysics* (Heidegger 1985, p. 76).

This capacity to pursue the interrupted emancipation of *praxis–prattein* is indeed indispensable to confirming the dialectic structure and the dialogical–conversational intention of *practical reasoning*—in their constitutive relation with the existential dispositions affirmed in the *subject/subject* experience of *Lebenswelt* (involving a productive circle of finitude and trans-finitude, *auctoritas* and reason, tradition and rational discursivity)—, if not directly to warranting the dialectic between *general* and *particular*, *past* and *present*, *"old" (presupposed)* and *"new"* (Bubner 1990). With this reinvention of *phronêsis-prudentia*, capable of experiencing community validity as the context–correlate of a *praxis* (a praxis of interpretations–conversations, of arguments, of narratives, of judgments)... we have actually a territory that, now unequivocally cultivating an *internal* perspective (involving a committed participant), also appears to be very (plurally) inhabited... and offers Legal "Theory" (with the word *theory* finally appropriately... in quotation marks!) steps we are all familiar with.

Which steps (generating more *litiges* than genuine *differends*)? Those who invite us to assimilate the lessons of *Neue philosophische Hermeneutik* (Esser, Kaufmann, Hassemer) and very specific manifestations of practical–cultural narrativisms (Boyd White, Nussbaum) or even those who incite us to follow the challenge of a *neue Hinwendung zur Rhetorik* (Viehweg, Perelman, Neumann), but also those who (beyond these exemplary axes and recognizing their dangers!) encourage us to experience the steps of a jurisprudential interpretive stage (Dworkin) and a critical–reflexive "theory" (Castanheira Neves).

1.3 Reconstructing Plurality from the Perspective of the Relationship Between the Issue of Content and Its Unity (Legal System) and the Issue of Constitution–Manifestation (Sources of Law)

Let us focus on this last alternative (critical–reflexive "theory"): this is in fact a meta-dogmatic reflection that, being driven by an *internal perspective*, takes as its guiding problem a specific *testimony of plurality*, as well as a reconstruction of the corresponding pragmatic. This is in fact an approach I have been developing under the inspiration of Castanheira Neves's proposal and it is within this horizon (and its *jurisprudentialist* approach) that I intend to remain in the remainder of this chapter.

The *raison d'être* of the broad-stroke reconstruction that I began by sketching (and which has occupied me until now) was (is) not, however, solely in the purpose of reaching this shore and remaining there peacefully. As I have already mentioned, this "theory" aims at a critical reconstruction (if not directly a mapping) of the plurality that, with regard to conceptions of law, legal thinking, and legally relevant performance (realization), currently divides the interpretative communities of jurists. There are, however, two levels to consider here. If, on the one hand, it is unacceptable to limit this reconstructive exercise to the alternatives provided by *Legal Theory* qua tale—those we have just mentioned (*supra*, Sect. 1.2)—it is no less unthinkable, on the other hand, to forget that such alternatives (separate or combined) ultimately project themselves constitutively into the spectrum of interpretative possibilities to be taken into account, which obviously means conditioning, generating, or even shaping–determining the positions in question, their practical–cultural assumptions, their dominant categories of intelligibility, and their relative positions on the map. It is, therefore, as if we were considering the exercise of an alternative reflective trend concerning *Legal Theory*, which, by addressing *directly* the pragmatics of plurality in contemporary legal thinking (and seeking to explore this as exhaustively as possible), would not fail to *indirectly* develop a *responsible conversation* with all the other possible configurations of *Legal Theory* and the complex web of interactions that these construct.

Concerning this internal critical theory, there are in fact two preliminary questions to consider, which exemplarily imply *open-ended responses*. The first concerns the idiom to be used by the critical testimony and is, in this sense, inseparable from the clarification of a kind of *archetypal* or *aspirational* internal perspective.[15] The second, in turn, concerns the "grids" for grouping and distributing (for mapping) the proposals to be reconstituted (Linhares 2017, pp. 15–20). None of these questions will be here and now directly considered.

Regarding the first, it suffices to emphasize that the internal horizon to be invoked *bets* on a specific treatment of Law (of a *certain* law)—significantly *inscribed* in the *possibilities* of the Western Text—as a cultural artifact, i.e., as a nonuniversal (culturally plausible and civilizationally molded) answer to the universal (anthropologically necessary) problem of the institutionalization of a social order (Neves 2008, pp. 13–41 and 101–116). It is, unsurprisingly, a question of considering the *path of response* initiated, as a claim of autonomy–isolation, in the Roman civitas, with the

[15] In the sense that Nigel Simmonds (following Fuller) allows us to acknowledge: Simmonds (2007), pp. 51–56. So that the *identity features* to be reconstituted (concerning the autonomy, specificity and limits of juridical arenas, its goals and/or values, its general or specific practical cultural meaning, as well as the intentions of legal thinking) do not represent *all or nothing characteristics* but rather *guiding intentions* or constitutive *aspirations* or *promises* (eventually *commitments* or *desiderata*), "by reference to" which (as if in an exercise in gradations) past or present expressions and their institutional instances should permanently be "judged."

so-called "rise of the jurists" (Stein 2007, p. 4) and thus of highlighting (as a *project*, a *form of life*, and a *tradition*) its continuous (even though incessantly renewed, rewritten, and reinterpreted) process of institutionalization: this has actually to do with a community of intersubjectively comparable subjects–persons, a community which has its generating perspective in a microscopically conceived experience, and which, notwithstanding the variability of the macroscopic contexts, is thus illuminated by an unmistakable experience of *tertiality*, involving the prius of the controversy–case and the conversion of singularity into analogically determinable *concreteness* (Linhares 2020, 2025).

It is the perspective-*visée* demanded by this project, if not the internal commitment with its tradition or the incorporation of its form of life, notwithstanding its constitutive inseparability from a specifically located conception of Law and Legal thinking (Castanheira Neves' jurisprudentialism), which will ensure the necessary equidistance (but also the patterns of comparability) to the testimony of plurality that, as a careful dialogue with all other conceptions of Law, this critical–reflexive Legal "Theory" wants to build. Isn't this, however, a paradoxically composed challenge? I would say it isn't. This meta-dogmatic (internal) dialogue with contemporary legal thinking (critically mapping its circles of *litiges* and *différends*) will only actually be able to succeed if it deliberately manages (and to the extent that it manages) radicalizing its approach.

How, in what terms? Quite simply, by integrating contributions from other meta-dogmatic levels, starting with the one that involves an internal philosophical reflection *taken to the limit*. This means in fact daring to open questions or to formulate interrogative agendas that, without concessions, problematize (that clearly test) the plausibility, punctuality, and survival of the project, the way of life, or the tradition that the Western Text persistently identifies with Law (its practices and institutional situations). As if we were "living" *from the inside*, a radical reflection about a practical–cultural experience... and this reflection, as an intertwinement of *commitment* and *critic*, rewriting permanently its memory, dared to question the contemporary endurance or congruence of this experience (if not the meaning of its *argument of continuity*)... without avoiding the possibility of a negative answer (and the cultural humility that this possibility demands).

Regarding the exercise of diagnosing–mapping, even greater restraint is here and now required. It will suffice to recall that the map is drawn respecting the basic grid we owe to Castanheira Neves (the one that distinguishes the decisive axes of normativisms, functionalisms, and jurisprudentialisms), while subjecting it, however, to the exercises of division, specification, and correction (if not "falsification") that two other complementary grids—one holistic, highlighting the experience of the collective or the commune (opposing discourses of *societas* and discourses of the dialectics *societas/communitas*) and the other specific, focusing on the methodological problem of jurisdictio (opposing juridicist and open area discourses)—will make possible. The overlapping of these three layers and their various distribution criteria (seriously considered as relevance filters) generates, in fact, new distribution possibilities, which allow, for example, a productive expansion of the basic grid. Expanding it may certainly mean simply redefining the content of one of the axes:

for example, admitting that the jurisprudentialist trend should cover all contemporary reinventions of *phronêsis* and their juridically relevant projections (which would imply distinguishing between lato sensu and stricto sensu modalities of jurisprudentialism). Expanding it may, however, also mean adding new axes, thus assigning (always with justifiable criteria) autonomous territories, for example, to contemporary reinventions of *natural law theories*, to the multiple expressions of *narrativism* (or narrative rationality), and, *last but not least*, to explicit or implicit manifestations of *conventionalism* (these reconstituted as various developments of Hart's legacy). And all this without forgetting that these options (and their categories of intelligibility) are always provisional, opening the way for constant redesign...—which makes this approach a fascinating exercise (if not a *work in progress*).

In any case, it is now time to move on from these two core issues and the complex paths they impose. What follows is, therefore, merely a sampling or partial exemplification of the circle that interweaves the *critical testimony* and the *pragmatics of plurality*, explicitly (deliberately) concentrated on a very specific question of articulation. The objective is, in fact, to explore the articulation between two of the major themes traditionally attributed to *Legal Theory*—that of the content of Law in its systemic intelligibility (the question of the *Legal System*) and that of the constitution and manifestation of this same content in its effective practical–social or practical–community assimilation (the question of the *Sources of Law*)—, treating this articulation (of assumed connections and presumed differences) as if it were the counterpoint between two diverse arenas. The intention is in fact less to consider them as such than to discuss how they articulate, or rather, to acknowledge unmistakably different modes of articulation and the legacies they manifest: which, in any case, means already assuming a selective filter, excluding from the *game* to be considered (and from its plausible pragmatic outcome) every proposal that does not give (or provide) the content of the law a systemic intelligibility... This is the case with the voices that correspond to the hard core of material (pragmatic) functionalisms (and their assumed instrumentalism).

2 The Equilibrium Between a Normativistically Horizontal Conception of the *Legal System* and a Plural Theory of the *Sources of Law*: The Legacy of Savigny and the Reinterpretations Developed by *Naturhistorische Methode* and *Allgemeine Rechtslehre*

The first way of articulating the issues of the *Legal System* and the *Sources of Law* is one that we could say supported by a *thesis of relative autonomy or separation*, the culminating expression of which was assumed by Conceptual Jurisprudence's *Naturhistorische Methode* and explicitly corroborated (as well as meta-dogmatically worked out) by *Allgemeine Rechtslehre*. If, in contrast, we recall the solutions due to other well-known expressions of nineteenth-century positivism, namely, to Austin's command theory (determining–demarcating the content of law as an expression of legislative and jurisdictional auctority–potestas or their commands, respectively, *general and indefinite commands* and *occasional and particular commands*)[16] and to exegetical positivism (overlapping *normativism* and *legalism*, while reducing law as a *system of norms* to an expression of legislative power, mainly *subspecies codicis*)—both of them, notwithstanding their irreconcilable differences, consecrating *unitarian* (non-separable) configurations of the issues at stake (*systematic content/sources*)—, this thesis of *relative autonomy or separation* appears as a specific irreducible feature, not always sufficiently highlighted, of nineteenth-century German legal thinking and its powerful legacy.

2.1 *Productive Clarifications*

The immediate productive clarification that this *thesis* allows concerns the counterpoint *normativism/legalism*, while highlighting the specificity of *naturhistorischer wissenschaflischer Positivismus* as a way of thinking Law and its rational universality, which, being constitutively *normativist* (defending a *dogmatically relevant*, not purely *epistemological*, normativism),[17] is not however *legalist*—which, in this context, means persistently resisting the overlapping that *l'École de l'Exegèse* consecrated.[18]

In addition to allowing us to recognize the "specific place" of *Scientific Positivism* (or the heterogenous legacies that this movement assimilates), this clarification opens up however other analytical possibilities, beginning obviously with the opportunity to denounce or challenge the apparent *doing what comes naturally*, which protects the global conjugation of legalism and normativism (reciprocally diluting problems of constitution and content and its systemic re-elaboration). Is this however a productive or interesting contribution? I admit that it is, moderately though, since as far as the dissociation at stake is concerned, a certain reflexive context, combining instrumentalism and pragmatism, strengthened by a diagnosis of radical pluralism (at the limit of incommensurability), but also favored by the explosion of *Zweckprogramme* and by specific institutional situations attributable to

[16] "[A]ll judge-made law is the creature of the sovereign or state" (Austin 1873, pp. 96–97).

[17] This means in fact defending an experience of the legal system, which is unambiguously *unidimensional*, basing its "existence" (as a mode-of-"being" *in abstract*) on the category of intelligibility *Rechtsnorm* and on the rational (structurally hypothetical–conditional) self-subsistence of its universal (general, abstract, and formal) autonomous *ought-to-be* (Law as a system of norms-*ratio*). Concerning the identification of *Rechtnorm* with an abstract *Rechtssatz* (in the context of the so-called operation of *juristische Analyse*), *see* Jhering (1883), p. 334.

[18] This overlapping not only identified *loi* and *droit* but also assumed that this same *loi écrite et positive* should be rigorously taken as the "exclusive criterion" (excluding any other criterion, rule or canon) regarding the interpretative determination of juridically relevant "normative content" (Neves 1995, pp. 184–185).

the emergence of the Social State, has generously provided us, at least for the last half century (from Philipp Heck to Hans Albert) with eloquent examples of strictly legalistic conceptions that unequivocally reject the normativist mediation (or the formalist implications), when they do not assume an explicit anti-formalist agenda.

Isn't this also a precious opportunity to discuss the rigorous meaning that the signifier *postivismus* deserves independently of these two qualifications? Certainly it is, even though the answer to be pursued should not today be limited to the thematization of the *subject/object* structure and the claim of autonomy (as *positum*) with which the cognitive intentions protect this object (although under the internal fire that contemporary critical epistemology, namely with regard to the implications of techno-science, effectively imposes), rather requiring, now in the juridically relevant context, a careful exploration of at least *three* paths and the corresponding (imperativist, normativist, and conventionalist) positivistic trends (respectively illuminated by the categories of intelligibility *command*, *norm-ratio*, and *rule*).

Surely more *interesting* (all the more so since it can only be understood as a transversal specification of the previous ones and their thematic challenges) is, however, the reflexive opportunity to close the circle, acknowledging that it is possible and expectable to separate–distribute rigorously the qualifications *normativism* and *legalism*: the first as a conception or reconstitutive option concerning the content of Law and its claims to unity (admitting solutions of conceptual coherence or architectonic consistence), the second as a conception or constructive option concerning the sources of Law (but also admitting diverse conceptions of statutory law and its *Konditional-*, *Zweck-*, or *Relationalprogramme*).[19] This is actually a non-negligible distribution, to which very little attention has also been paid.

2.2 Heterogeneous Legacies and Surprising Circularities

What is the origin of this *separation thesis* (better saying, of this *articulation* through *separation*), and what are its implications? Its origin is evidently the fertile tension between two heterogeneous worlds, their practical and cultural horizons, and their categories of intelligibility. I am referring, of course, to the tension (in the limit of incommensurability) between *historicism* and *normativism*, i.e., between a configuration of the material substance of Law (*Rechtsstoff*) as a manifestation of the peculiarity and particularism of a specific community (given by the *total past* of the nation and based on the *Volksgeist*) (Neves 1995, pp. 203–214) and an experience of the conjugation (if not intertwinement) between the claims of *juridicity* and *scientificity* (treating *wissenshaftlich* as *juristisch* and *juristisch* as *wissenschaftlich*) that only the explicit or implicit recognition of the "rational nature" of Law (*als Vernunftmäßigkeit des Rechts*) (Fikentscher 1976, p. 91, note 12—quoting Puchta), justified by the universality of *systemic intentions*, will ultimately allow.

[19] *See* infra, note 59.

We are once again faced with a territory of manifest complexity, admitting distinct conceptions of historicity and "historical development," as well as diverse representations of the so-called systemic intentions. There is, however, an indisputable convergence, which we can synthesize by distinguishing a common core of intelligibility. This shared *Inbegriff* is precisely that in which the *System*—identified with the "rational" anticipation of a logical–abstract unity—offers itself, so to speak, "in its proper sense" (*im eigentlich Sinn, als Systematisierungskriterium*): as the condition of possibility (and simultaneously the criterion) of an exposition (selection, ordering, and classification–distribution) of contingent material-data, which, by providing these data with a rationally intelligible position-*Stellung* (capable of converting them into legal propositions, i.e., abstrakte *Rechtssätze*, if not *Rechtsätze* tout court), but above all, by respecting–revealing the *coherence by identity* (by *noncontradiction*) of the corresponding content (Neves 1995, pp. 155–157)—by allowing their meanings to be recognized–recreated in their "higher stages of aggregation," as Institutes and Concepts (*[als] Erhebung des Rechtsstoffes in einen höhern Aggregatzustand*) (Jhering 1883, p. 361)—ends up imposing itself also and inseparably as the *condition–criterion* of the *perspective–"subject"* and the simultaneous claims to *scientificity* and *juridicity* that distinguish it.

Since it is impossible to allude here, even schematically, to the various configurations of this tension[20] and the dialectics (at the unconfessable limit of circularity) that attenuates it, I will try to clarify a little more the proposed integrative solution, using exclusively Jhering's mediation (mobilizing the scheme that his proposition stabilizes): I am obviously referring to the *Theorie der juristischen Technik* proposed in the second part of the *Geist des römischen Rechts* and most especially to the systematization of "tasks"-*Aufgabe* (and "purposes"-*Zwecke*) proposed in § 38 ("*Die Aufgabe der Technik und die Mittel zu ihrer Lösung im Allgemeinen*") (Jhering 1883, pp. 322–333). Among other things, this privileged mediation helps to clarify that the solution in question is constructed by exploring two separations–splits and the unitary structure that, without paradox, these splits generate. Which splits are those? The one that separates Law and legal thinking... but also the one that opposes–articulates a certain (contingent) given *object* and the (systematic) *perspective–"subject"* that rationalizes it: in such a way that the elements of the first split can occupy the spaces opposed–articulated by the second...—which means legitimizing a certain given law (to be known) as an object of legal thinking and this one as a *dogmatic science of law*.

We may begin by clarifying that the "object" Law (the ensemble of the law materials treated as an o*bject* in its immediate pre-systematic rough manifestation), notwithstanding the contingent particularism that is expected to characterize it, becomes analytically intelligible through the anticipated (circular) projection of a *theory of sources*: the one that is implicit in Savigny's *drei Rechtsarten* (*Gewohnheitsrecht, Gesetzesrecht, Juristenrecht*). This typification circumscribes

[20] *See* exemplarily Brockmöller (1997), p. 83, p. 114, and pp. 125–130 (« *Das Rechtssystem—Drei Systeme des Rechts* »).

in fact the set of permitted material-data, immediately including (in a first and irreducible dual front) the Law that is "posited" (*positum*) and the Law that is "imposed" (*prescribed*), the first emerging from customary experience, the second from legislative production, both of them attributable to the (historical–communitarian) "political element" (*Der Kürze wegen nennen wir künftig den Zusammenhang des Rechts mit dem allgemeinen Volksleben das politische Element, das abgeſonderte wissenschaftliche Leben des Rechts aber das technische Element desselben*).[21]

Taking into account the components of nineteenth-century German legal thinking, namely the dimension directly emerging from its *Pandektendogmatik*, is certainly also treating as law-object the *Digesta*'s materials. Now with less visible (or less compulsive) autonomy, certainly because those *Corpus Juris Civilis*'s texts, celebrated as *Incarnation des absoluten Rechtsgedankens* or simply assimilated as an indispensable foreign Law, appear to be inscribed on the border between the "political element" and the "technical element" (or the arenas that these elements construct): as if, at least tendentially, they (certainly not by chance treated as *Rechtsgedänke* or *Rechtssätze*) were less separable[22] from the full performance of the *perspective–"subject"* and its development as *dogmatische Rechtswissenschaft*. And yet, this same typification excludes jurisdiction as such, which means that the *Rechtsart* named *Juristenrecht* (by focusing on the scientific–dogmatic dimension, if not on the *learned jurist*, as the bearer of the *Volksgeist*) does not justify the treatment of jurisdiction as an authentic source of Law. Is this a manifestation of the institutional (Roman–Germanic or civil law) context? Apparently, it is.

To understand the weight related with this institutional dimension (*common law* versus *civil law*), it suffices recalling the role that (especially through the reflection developed by the *Allgemeine Rechtslehre*) is played by the counterpoint with common law analytical (imperative) positivism: concerning customary and jurisdictional experiences or their role as sources of law, a singular inversion actually operates here, with imperative positivism vigorously rejecting the first one and treating the decisions of the second as commands (*law made judicially, or in the way of improper legislation*),[23] with normative positivism (now through its metadogmatic approach) rejecting the second one and consecrating the first (*Die Bedeutung einer verbindliche Norm für gerichtliche Entscheidung kann einer Regel*

[21] Cf. Savigny (1814), p. 12.

[22] Or, if you like, more circularly inseparable… It's in fact all a matter of gradation (and difference in degree).

[23] "By many of the admirers of customary laws (and, especially, of their German admirers), they are thought to oblige legally (independently of the sovereign or state), *because* the citizens or subjects have observed and kept them. (…) [B]efore it is adopted by the courts and clothed with the legal sanction, [the costum] (…) is [however] merely a rule of positive morality (…) [,] a rule generally observed by the citizens or subjects (…). [W]hen costumes are turned into legal rules by decisions of subject judges, the legal rules which emerge from the costumes are *tacit* commands of the sovereign legislature (…). My present purpose is merely this: to prove that the positive law styled *customary* (and all positive law made judicially) is establish by the state directly or circuitously, and therefore, is *imperative*…" (Austin 1872, pp. 103, 104, 105).

des Herkommens durch ein Gesetz, sowie durch die Macht des Herkommens und der in ihm wirksamen Überzeugungen *selbst zuerkannt sein*).[24]

And yet, there are other reasons to be considered. As might be expected, adherence to a "modern conception of state" and the principle of separation of powers (under the explicit modus operandi of the *Rechtstaat*) entails the requirement to view the courts as organs of enforcement, not of creation and positivization of legal propositions.[25]

The context of justification does not end here, however. There is in fact a deeper reason, "unconfessable" insofar as it compromises the epistemological rigor of the subject/object split. Recognizing an autonomous force in custom does not, in fact, result exclusively from contingent characteristics manifested in the given object; it is also an integral part of the perspective-*subject* and the experiences of *historicity* it assimilates. Moreover, it gives us a clue (a cue) to decipher the dynamic of circularity that hides behind this implacable structure: as if what promised to be a cognitively rigorous approach turned out to be an intertwinement of reciprocal anticipations and projections.

To conclude, we will highlight this circularity, alluding first to the conception of the *legal system*, then to the *theory of sources*: regarding the former, focusing once again on Jhering's systematization; regarding the latter, alluding very briefly to one of the disputes that divides Bergbohm and Merkel.

Let us begin with the decisive role of *lower jurisprudence* (*niedere Jurisprudenz*) addressing the so-called *law-object*, already available in contingent ordering structures (historically real institutions, organic orders, collections, codes, repeated practices), in order to transform it into an authentic *objective law*, which means making it rationally "knowable"—capable of constituting an authentic *epistemological objectum* (dominated by the self-subsistent model of the norm–*ratio* and the ordering possibilities it sustains). As we know, this conversion of all materials into abstract *Rechtssätze* is the task of "analysis," seriously taken as the legal "art" of separation–delimitation (*juristische Scheidekunst*). According to Jhering, it is a matter of revealing the "chemically" simplest elements of law (*die einfachen Elemente des Rechts)* (Jhering 1883, p. 335) and thus of fulfilling an exercise of autonomization of the "abstract" (*das Moment der Allgemeinheit*) (Jhering 1883, p. 336), which is also an exercise of dissociation–division (pp. 336 and 343–344)—the one that distinguishes those "elements" or "parts" that should be recognized as "abstract or general" from all those that can be called "individual" or "concrete," if

[24] Cf. Merkel (1885), p. 66 (§ 114).

[25] «Im modernen Staate ist für die bezeichnete schöpferische Tätigkeit der Gerichte nur ein geringer Spielraum gegeben. Dieselbe sehen sich hier einem ausgebildeten, im umfassenden Gestzeswerfen (Kodifikationen) fixierten Recthte gegenüber, dessen Fortbildung dem Gestezgeber, nicht ihnen zufällt. Sie sind Organe der Anwendung, nicht der "Setzung" (Schaffung) der Rechtssätze. Diese scharfe Scheidung von Rechtssetzung und Rechtsanwendung, und die Beschränkung der Gerichte auf die letzere (...), setz eine hohe Entwicklung des objektiven Rechts und der staatlichen Einrichtungen (...) voraus...» (Merkel 1885, pp. 69–70, § 119).

not "local" or "special" (*Ihr Zweck ist (...) Klarstellung dessen, was in Wirklichkeit individuell und in Wirklichkeit allgemein ist*) (Jhering 1883, pp. 336–337).

In this separation we will in fact have a manifestation of "progress" or "improvement" (*Fortbildung*) (Jhering 1883, p. 341) that simultaneously (circularly!) concerns Law and legal thinking and that is thus celebrated as an "evolutionary process" (*[als] Entwicklungsgeschichte*) (p. 338). In this sequence of tasks, we certainly cannot forget "logical concentration" (*die logische Konzentration*) (pp. 352–357) and "construction–systematization" (*die juristische Konstruktion*) (pp. 357–420), the former still fulfilled by "lower jurisprudence", the latter already occupying "higher jurisprudence", which we shall not consider here. In any case, the components that these tasks allow us to obtain (respectively, the *general principles of law* and the network of *institutes* and *concepts*) are no longer integral parts of the *content* of law itself, but rather conditions of possibility or epistemological resources of the perspective-*subject* (also here without preventing well-known manifestations of circularity!). It is also no coincidence that, despite living in a time of effervescent emergence of constitutionalism, this conception of the system preserves a horizontal intelligibility (it is a system of norms, one next to the other, explored in their *neighboring relationships*), capable of fully abstracting from the source that gave rise to each of them (the component *potestas* and the category command do not interfere in the configuration of the system!)... and finding in the network of concepts and institutes its solution of unity (through categorical–classificatory *coherence*).

The same concern with the articulation between the unity of the system and the plurality of the sources, however, also leads us to the theme of the theory *encore à faire* that dominated the "project" of the *Allgemeine Rechtslehre*. There is indeed a common solution of equilibrium, but there are also exemplary divergences. The solution (shared by Merkel, Bergbohm, and Bierling)[26] is one that, based on Savigny's three *Rechtsarten*, explicitly rejects the idea that the last (*Juristenrecht*) can be seen as a "material source": which allows to recognize, by contrast, that the "original order" of custom and the "second-degree order" of legislation (Bierling) constitute two absolutely irreducible juridical "ways of being"... and that remain irreducible, despite the diminishment of the meaning of customary law that the process of the institutionalization of the State or the statist tendency (with the organization of powers that this requires) has progressively imposed.

The divergence is explicitly triggered by Bergbohm, who argues (versus Merkel) the need for a new theory of customary law: this theory should in fact be "freed" from the circle of the *Historiker* or from the compromises that their legacy continues to impose... in order to effectively aspiring to develop the possibilities of a *Rechtsform*, which may be combined with a renewal of the *principle of historicity* (Bergbohm 1892–1973, pp. 22–23, 63, 517, note 44 and pp. 546–549).[27] Isn't this

[26] Cf. Merkel (1885), pp. 65–69; Bierling (1887–Bierling 1965), pp. 95–97; Bergbohm (1892-1973), pp. 521–525.

[27] For a development, clarifying the place of this proposal, *see* Linhares (2009), pp. 303–306.

an aspiration that culminates in the promise of a *new theory of sources*? We can say it is (Bergbohm 1892–1973, pp. 548–552). Above all, however, it is an aspiration that opens disturbing doors, significantly wounding the normativist understanding that sustains this meta-dogmatic purification (Linhares 2009). More exemplarily than ever, we are here, in fact, exposed to the intertwining of law-*objec*t and perspective-*subject*, but now to threaten the equilibrium by differentiation between the problem of the system and the problem of the sources.

3 The Equilibrium Between a Conventionalist Conception of the *Rule* and the Contingent Plurality Justified by the Thesis of *Social Sources*: The Challenges of Soft Positivism (and Its Legacy)

With the (no less complex) world of *conventionalist positivism* (in its broadest sense, involving, as we already know, the legacy of Hart's *rule of recognition* and its diverse developments), the articulation between the content of law and its constitution (between the *experience of the "system"* and the *question of sources*) is significantly another, now supported by an idea of *full overlap* or *reciprocal identification*: in two words, this means that the content of law will be the one that its social sources contingently determine it to be (*the social fact source thesis*), or, more accurately, that... when we consider the problem of identifying existent law and the *constituens* of legal content (or, in the words of Raz, the problem of "reasoning about what the law is"),[28] the only permitted answer is certainly the one which, in making a claim for the existence conditions of legal normativity, confirms *the indispensable mediation* of a "conventional" *rule of recognition* "specifying the sources of law and the relationships of superiority and subordination holding between them"[29]—without forgetting that this major secondary Rule should be experienced as "a form of judicial customary rule existing only if it is accepted and practised in the law-identifying and law-applying operations of the courts,"[30] thus offering itself (as an "empirical, though complex, question of fact"[31]) inseparable from the *social*

[28] "Reasoning about what the law is, reasoning to the conclusion that the content of law is such and such, reasoning whose sole premises are that the law is such and such and whose (...) conclusions merely state the content of existing law." (Raz 2009, pp. 376–379).

[29] Hart (1994), pp. 266, 268.

[30] Hart (1994), p. 256.

[31] "The question whether a rule of recognition exists and what its content is, i.e. what the criteria of validity in any given legal system are, is regarded throughout this book as an empirical, though complex, question of fact. This is true even though it is also true that normally, when a lawyer operating within the system asserts that some particular rule is valid he does not explicitly state but tacitly presupposes the fact that the rule of recognition (by reference to which he has tested the validity of the particular rule) exists as the accepted rule of recognition of the system. If challenged, what is thus presupposed but left unstated could be established by appeal to the facts, i.e.

practices, which, in each legal order, simultaneously follow, determine, and fix it, and from those practices in their constitutive connection with the legal (law-identifying and law-applying) officials' internal point of view ("acceptance of the rule of recognition from the internal point of view by officials is a conceptual requirement of the possibility of law").[32]

Which, returning to the beginning, authorizes us to a new reformulation in two words, this one to emphasize that the overlapping relationship between the question of the *content of the law* and the question of the *sources* (or between the answers to those questions in each legal order) is due to the full convergence (or equilibrium) between the *social fact (source) thesis* (*only social facts determine the content of law*) and the *conventionality thesis* (*the claim that law is made possible by an inter-dependent convergence of behavior and attitude*)—if not also between these and the so-called *discretion thesis* (as an implication of the *open texture of law*). The transparency of this solution (defended as true common ground) nevertheless requires some specifications, as well as it admits very different developments (with truly irreconcilable *endpoints*).

3.1 Specifying the Overlapping Thesis

Regarding the specifications, it suffices to confirm that the term *conventionalism* appears here in its broadest sense, identifying a conception of Law that, concerning the issue of juridical *content*, claims the "necessity" of "social facts" (treated either directly, as determinants, or indirectly, as determinants of the determinants, of this content),[33] or more specifically, a conception of Law that claims the full dependence of its content—highlighted through the category de intelligibility *rule*—on contingent practices of judicial consensus (with outcomes that, in different legal orders, can be radically diverse). The role played by the category *rule*—in contrast with two categories that we have met before (*command* and *norm*), but also as an integral (nondiscriminated) expression of normativity (which as such does not allow a *binominal* composition with *principles*)—confers on this content a minimum of systematicity—contrasting with the unsystematic character attributable to a pure juxtaposition (or ensemble) of commands: a minimum of systematicity, however, which in turn operates less as a claim of unity (by consistency or coherence)—as it happens with the category *norm*—than as the corroboration of a shared and repeated use of "general classificatory words." As we know, these words are assimilable as such (in their universality claims) from an *internal perspective*, admitting an use

to the actual practice of the courts and officials of the system when identifying the law which they are to apply" (Hart 1994, pp. 292–293).

[32] Coleman (2001), p. 76.

[33] I am obviously alluding to Coleman's formulations: see Coleman (2009) p. 359 and pp. 384–386 ("*Reformulating ILP*").

that can oscillate between a maximum or minimum intensity... and thus allowing a plural spectrum of normative expressions.[34]

In this context (and with this common ground), *conventionalism stricto sensu* corresponds to a specification of the *thesis of conventionality*—and in this sense to a position in the global conventionalist field supported only by some of the interlocutors (and explicitly rejected by others): I refer to a specification that conceives of the practices of "identifying," "interpreting," and "applying" legal contents as a *shared cooperative interaction* (among persons over a period of time), while admitting that it may happen a "fundamental and penetrating disagreement about how to continue this activity" (*officials can and do disagree (...) about what [the rule] (...) requires of them (...) and this is perfectly compatible with the rule of recognition regulating a conventional practice, and thus with the rule of recognition being a conventional rule*).[35] As if the rule of recognition could be treated as a parameter of interaction permanently reinterpreted and this particular accentuation of the components "behavior" and "attitude" (eventually extended to the decisions and choices of ordinary citizens) gained reflexively with a critical dialogue with Hume's and Lewis's legacies, opening the door to a juridically relevant *theory of conventions* (Coleman, Marmor, Postema, den Hartogh, Gilbert).[36]

3.2 *Two Promising Internal Grids*

As for the various developments, and despite the appreciable contributions they promise for a pragmatics of plurality, this is not the time to dwell on the disputes that (always with considerable repercussions on non-positivist fronts) these developments foment in the positivist camp. It will suffice mentioning two internal *grids*, certainly not to explore them in detail, but to ask which components of those grids (in their explicit counterpoint) most coherently correspond to the guiding thesis of overlapping or identification between *legal content* and *legal sources*.

3.3.2.1 The first grid is inevitably the one that, doing justice to the most significant of the controversies that divide Hart's heirs (the counterpoint between *exclusive* and *inclusive–incorporationist* positivisms), distinguishes between a *separation thesis* (*legality and morality are* necessarily *separate from one another*) and a *separability thesis* (*legality and morality are only separable, not necessarily separate*).[37] It is indispensable to add that the strong *separation thesis*, notwithstanding the diversity of the conjugated voices (Raz, Shapiro, Marmor), generates an univocal common ground, assumed as *exclusive positivism*, while the *separability thesis* justifies in turn two plausible versions (and their interne gradations): a defense of *sepa-*

[34] Hart (1994), pp. 124–125.

[35] Cf. Coleman (2021), pp. 157–158.

[36] For a development, *see* Postema (2011), pp. 483–545.

[37] Cf. Waluchow (2006).

rability only as *inclusion* (Waluchow)—which means arguing that one of the possible conditions of juridically relevant validity, inscribed as such in the rule of recognition (and thus contingently identified and "applied" by the practice of legal officials), corresponds directly and exclusively to a claim of conformity with moral principles (*moral values and principles count among the possible grounds that a legal system might accept for determining the existence and content of valid laws (…), a legal system's rule(s) of recognition [can] contain explicitly moral tests or criteria for the legal validity of (…) legislation*)[38]; a defense of *separability* not only as *inclusion* (in the sense that we have just considered) but also as *incorporation*, either a *moderate* (Kramer) or a *robust* (Coleman) one—which means admitting that certain moral principles, in specific contexts and under certain conditions, may acquire juridical force (being as such self-subsistently invoked as binding Law) only for reasons related to their own "worthiness," that is, their "correctness" or "soundness" as moral requirements… and in such a way that this "merit" appears as the only "test" on which their authoritative force depends (*a legal system can be structured by a Rule of Recognition which effectively establishes that correctness as a moral precept is sufficient to render a norm binding as a law*).[39]

As far as the mapping effect is concerned, the question addressed to the (greater or lesser) coherence of these different approaches (as conceptions or experiences of the Rule of Recognition) regarding the thesis of overlapping or identification (between the content of law and the contingent variable answer due to the social sources) may prove to be especially productive. Not because we are able to obtain an answer that is unequivocal or unique. Rather, because we acknowledge here an analytically reversible web of arguments that sheds significant light on the different positions.

If, for instance, in order to understand the thesis of *social sources*, we focus on the commonly accepted constitutive character of the practices of legal officials (treating the rule of recognition simultaneously as a governing and guiding normative *context* and a factual *correlate* of the convergent social practices and their reflective attitude of acceptance), the positions supported by *inclusive positivists* actually appear to be the most coherent… and with a degree of coherence that is accentuated when we move from inclusivism tout court to moderate incorporationism and from this one to robust incorporationism: if, in a given legal order, these contingent practices confer legal intelligibility and force to a certain moral content or to the principle that specifies it (and for reasons that have to do exclusively with the merit of this content), respect for the factual dimension seems actually to require accepting without further ado (or problematization) the possibility of particular legal orders in which following, determining and fixing the Rule validates an effective *inclusion* of moral tests or criteria, if not an authentic *incorporation* of moral principles. This means that it seems less consistent with the full acceptance of the factual dimension to defend the introduction of more restrictive *criteria* (rejecting

[38] Waluchow (1994), p. 82.

[39] Kramer (2004), p. 25.

the relevance of some of the practices and thus selecting a factuality *with conditions*). Which criteria? Precisely those that require (without exception) the mediation of authority-potestas and the corresponding enactment or pedigree tests (*exclusive positivism*). Or those that attribute to moral contents an exclusive role of external warrants or grounds (*inclusive positivism tout court*). Or even those that exhaust (reduce) the relevance of moral tests to the scope of *hard cases* (*moderate incorporationism*).

But is this necessarily the case, however? There is in fact another powerful side to this web, capable (almost seamlessly) of generating a flow of opposing arguments. These can for instance begin with the conclusion-claim that considering the social source thesis does not mean considering a pure factuality, but rather corroborating a *juridically relevant* factuality (if not an institutional reality). And if it is so, shouldn't the respect for the specific relevance of these social facts actually imply some necessary distinctions and the corresponding demarcation exercises? Which demarcation exercises?

The first is certainly the one which, according to Raz, allows us to distinguish between the problem of "reasoning about law" (culminating in an autonomous juridical conclusion on the content of law) and the problem of "reasoning according to law" ("reasoning about how legal disputes should be settled according to law"), this one obviously including the issue of *specific judicial reasoning*, with its contextualized interpretation (Raz 2009, pp. 376–379): while the first of these problems excludes the participation of *moral tests*; the second (highlighted by the *discretion thesis*) mobilizes in fact, explicitly, a *non-incorporated morality* (*even judges are humans (...), in being human, they are subject to morality*).[40] This is not however the unique demarcation exercise allowed. Fully preserving the distinction between juridicity and morality, there is certainly the possibility of defending, with Waluchov (here closely following Hart), that moral contents may, in certain legal orders, perform a warranting or grounding role relevant for juridical normativity while remaining entirely *free from incorporation* (inclusivism tout court).[41] As there is finally the one that allows *incorporation* but under the sign of exceptionality, reserving it for methodological situations of *hard cases* (*the place is correctly characterized as the domain of exceptionality rather than the domain of tipicality*).[42,43]

This apparent continuity–complicity between exclusionary and inclusivist arguments (in a surprising common front that chooses Coleman's *robust incorporationism* as its critical target)[44] has, moreover, an eloquent expression in the so-called debate (*le litige...*) about the practical difference ("legal rules must, in principle, be

---

[40] Cf. Raz (2009), pp. 183–190 (« *Even Judges are Humans* »).

[41] "[M]oral values and principles count among the possible grounds that a legal system might accept for determining the existence and content of valid laws (...), a legal system's rule(s) of recognition [can] contain explicitly moral tests or criteria for the legal validity of (...) legislation" (Waluchow 1994, p. 82).

[42] Cf. Kramer (2004), p. 64.

[43] Cf. Kramer (2004), pp. 59–64 (« *What Happens in Hard Cases* »).

[44] To consider Coleman's eloquent position, *see* mainly Coleman (2005).

capable of securing conformity by making a difference to an agent's practical reasoning").[45] It is as if we had here two complementary opponent approaches (one exclusionary, the other inclusivist),[46] both contributing to specify the meaning of stability (or stabilizing practices), both resisting the seductions of *robust incorporationism*, while denouncing the dangers of a "pronouncement" which, establishing "moral worthiness" as "the *lone* sufficient condition for the status of norms as legal norms" (in every case, not only in hard cases), would concede a dangerous (uncontrollable) "elasticity" to recognitional practice—an elasticity which, confronted with the conditions of contemporary plural (fragmented, heterogeneous) societies, would paradoxically prevent a plausible distinction between *content* and *extension* and would condemn us to extreme *casuistry* (as if the Major Rule instructed "officials to handle every case by applying the moral norms that produce the optimal result in the circumstances").[47]

3.3.2.2 A second grid is explicitly introduced by Coleman (2011, pp. 56–72) while exploring what he calls a *second-order view* or a *meta-semantic* (or *meta-metaphysic*) *level*: distinguishing itself from a first possible level, called semantic (*a first-order, object-level view*), which is concerned with answering the question "what determines legal content?", this second level faces the following question: "what determines the determinants of legal content?" or "what are the grounds of the determinants of legal content?"

---

[45] Cf. Shapiro (2000), p. 129.

[46] The first approach is introduced by Shapiro (as a defense of *practical difference*) in order to reject the arguments of inclusive positivism ("moral rules validated by an inclusive rule of recognition cannot be action guiding in the manner in which legal rules are supposed to be action guiding") (Phillips 2011, p. 4)—which means reconstituting the complex relationship between law and morality (necessarily separated when we identify law's content, necessarily connected when we consider law's claim to a specific legal point of view) (Shapiro 2011, pp. 186–188) ("*The Legal Point of View*") and paving the way not only for the identification of social planning with pedigreed norms (indispensable in grasping the old/new dynamics) but also, in particular, for the decisive understanding of law's guidance as *planning* ("the legal rules of a particular system are just the general plans, or plan-like norms"), whose "logic" would be violated if a moral "deliberation on the merits" was constitutively allowed (Shapiro 2009, pp. 329 and 334).

The second approach corresponds to the rejection of *practical difference* (i.e., to the rejection of this difference as an authentic conceptual claim) justified both by *inclusivism tout court* and *moderate incorporationism*, in a way that reconciles Waluchow and Kramer (versus Coleman)—while arguing that compliance with morality or conformity with moral principles should be understood as a "necessary" ("though insufficient") "condition of validity" (Waluchow 2000, pp. 45 ff.). This argument gives Kramer the opportunity to restore the practical difference as a "plurative and partly empirical claim" (confining "moral precepts" as "non-source-based norms" to the "domain of exceptionality" of "hard cases")—which, here and now (and still versus Coleman), certainly means corroborating the central thesis of *moderate incorporationism* that legal officials' disagreements, even when they are about application, may introduce a significant measure of irregularity into practices and, as such, compromise (sacrifice) not only the efficiency but also the existence of an authentic legal order ("a fairly substantial degree of regularity is essential not just for the efficiency of a legal regime, but also for its very existence as such") (Kramer 2004, pp. 27, 28, 59–64). See also Linhares 2016, pp. 429–432.

[47] Kramer (2004), p. 29.

Exclusionary positivism disputes (as one of the possible conceptions) the first level, answering its question directly with the *social sources thesis* (*only social facts determine the content of law*)... and thus competing only with *non-positivisms* (here identified with *natural law approaches*)—those that (in stronger or weaker terms) defend that such determinants are (exclusively or not) normative facts *(only normative, evaluative, or moral facts contribute to the content of law/both normative and social facts contribute to legal content)*. Inclusive positivism, by arguing that the determinants of determinants are merely social facts—even when the content of law is determined by moral tests (which, as we know, is an effective possibility to be taken into account!)—, situates its claims in contrast at the meta-semantic level... thus competing no longer with exclusionary positivism and non-positivisms... but with two other possible interlocutors, which Coleman identifies mobilizing the "masks" of *normativism* and *conceptualism* (*inclusive legal positivism, normativism, and conceptualism are all competing accounts at the metalevel: putative accounts of how it is that these facts (...) and not others (...) contribute to legal content*).[48] It should be added that *normativism* at this meta-semantic level (in stronger or weaker versions) corresponds to all positions in which the determinants of determinants are (or can be) normative facts (*normative facts determine the determinants of legal content*)... and that *conceptualism*, in contrast, qualifies all those others in which the so-called fundamental determinants are confused with presumably true propositions "about the essential nature" of legality (*the determinants of legal content derive from truths about the essential nature of law*).[49]

The separation of these levels and the compossibility of the two maps they engender (with the internal gradations that the claims of necessity or mere contingency invariably add to the interlocutors we have already considered) open up surprising possibilities for classification: for Coleman, it is not, in fact, simply a matter of giving renewed strength to the hard core of his proposal—finally justifying why the semantic thesis of social sources proves to be fully compatible with the meta-semantic thesis of the incorporation of moral principles (notwithstanding the fact that the former often appears to us illuminated by a claim of necessity and the latter imposes itself on us predominantly associated with a claim of possibility or contingency)—it is also a matter of being able to show that the combinations are multiple... and that perspectives that are fundamentally convergent at the semantic level (after all, all those that frequent the positivist camp!) can diverge significantly at the meta-semantic level... According to this grid, only Coleman's perspective would be able to sustain an authentic *inclusive positivism* (capable of assuming a claim of contingency... but above all of rejecting that the effective incorporation of principles could be associated with any type of fundamental claims about the *nature of law*)... and only Shapiro's approach would in turn be able to take seriously a pure *conceptualism* (justified by the categories of intelligibility *social planning* and *moral aim*, defended on a purely categorical, non-normative level).

---

48 Coleman (2011), p. 71.

49 For a detailed dialogue with this grid, *see* Linhares (2013), pp. 96–103.

As for Hart and Raz, it is as if they already assumed hybrid meta-semantic positions, the former corresponding to an overlap of *inclusivism* (in a necessary version) and conceptualism (illuminated by the category *rule of recognition*), and the latter resulting from an effective compromise between *conceptualism* and *normativism*—with conceptualism imposing itself through the understanding of the nature of law as authority… and with normativism already corresponding to the exploration of the morality or moral nature of this claim (*as a claim to superior service*) or of the arguments that support it, in their critical-regulative specificity (*Raz holds that the determinants of legal content derive from claims about the essential nature of law, but at least some of those claims are, in his account, defended on normative grounds*) (Coleman 2011, pp. 74–75).

In any case, the solution that interests us here once again distinguishes (isolates) Coleman's proposal… corroborating the conclusion that a pure or hybrid conceptualist view always diminishes the strength or coherence of the thesis of the overlap between the problems of the system and the sources. This means that the most coherent perspective (capable of guaranteeing this overlap in all its purity) will thus be an anti-conceptualist approach (rejecting the selection or restriction or supplementary condition that the features regarding the *nature of law* necessarily introduce). This gives special meaning to the assertion that legal content is fully determined by the institutionally consecrated modes of constitution–manifestation–positivation of legality, while the question of so-called *legal semantics* (as a *semantics of legal discourse*) is an entirely different one, since it claims an authentic *theory of meaning*.

We have here, in fact, another world of productive distinctions, which, once again, we will refrain from entering! This restraint does not, however, preclude a final question: Could it be that the resistance to pure overlapping isn't ultimately in the category of intelligibility *rule* itself and in the way (through the claim of generality associated with its classificatory words) this category preserves (albeit only partially) the heritage of the category norm-*ratio*? This question provides in fact the cue we need to move on to a third configuration of the *system/sources* relationship.

4 Exposing *Legal Theory* to the Possibilities of an Internal Perspective: Paying Attention to the Multidimensionality of the *Legal System* and the Plurality of (Institutionalized or Quasi-Institutionalized) Sources

The path offered by this third possibility brings us "back" to a solution of relative autonomy between the problem of the content and the problem of the constitution of law "in force" (and/or the responses they authorize). The way this autonomy is conceived of and the corresponding articulation solution are, however, radically different from those consecrated by nineteenth-century normativism (and pursued by other formalisms). It is, in fact, a matter of taking seriously an internal, explicitly practical–normative perspective (and the *commitment to juridicity* that this *participant point of view* demands) and, in this way, of defending that each *phenomenological–normative* approach to the problem of the sources of Law (capable of fully respecting, in each positive legal order, the historical–social specificity of its process of constitution) (Neves 1995, pp. 8–15) should effectively allow (or should productively be intertwined with) a multidimensional experience of its unitarian content (capable of identifying this system as one of the necessary dimensions of specifically juridical rationality) (Neves 1995, pp. 165–180).

4.1 The Internal Perspective

This conjugation and intertwinement mobilize a *non-positivist conception* of Law, which in a first approach, we could persuasively identify with Dworkin's interpretivism and with the "lesson" developed by *Justice in Robes*, attributing to *General Theory of Law* (sic) a simultaneously critical–philosophical and practical–normative identity (*[exploring] the concept of "the law" of some place or entity being to a particular effect (...) [claiming] about what the law requires or prohibits or creates (...), [asking] what rights and duties the system recognises*),[50] while assuming the centrality of a *doctrinal concept* and its internal interpretive experience—an experience that, being built in diverse stages (*semantic*, *jurisprudential*, *doctrinal* stricto sensu, *adjudicative* stages),[51] is significantly supported by the normatively integrative horizon of the *community of principles.*

And yet, to understand this distinction, followed by a solution of conjugation and intertwinement, it is not enough to require a non-positivist conception, even when this one unequivocally combines (as it happens with Dworkin) an aspirational perspective and a substantive determination, i.e., when it claims that the guiding aspirations or normative practical commitments that identify (distinguish) Law as an autonomous (unmistakable) branch of *political morality*—here explicitly principles... in their constitutive connection with legal rights (Dworkin 2011, p. 404)—should be determined and concretized through a dominantly material or substantive interpretative discourse.

To fully understand this distinction and its implications, it is indispensable here to return to the approach that, in regard with the diverse modes of expansion of *Legal Theory*, we have already identified as a critical–reflexive one (supra, 1.3.): an approach that we saw as a plausible projection of a jurisprudentialist conception of Law and which thus combines a non-positivist substantive intelligibility with an explicit refusal of a *culturally neutral* experience of Law (i.e., of the dominant flow that, more implicitly than explicitly, goes on sustaining this a-cultural representation), which means, on the positive side, daring a full practical–cultural

[50] Dworkin (2006), p. 02.

[51] Dworkin (2006), p. 09 and ss.

civilizational contextualization, with identifiable conditions of emergence and diverse cycles of institutionalization (freed from claims of a-cultural universality or ontological or onto-anthropological necessity) and with it, assuming conclusion-claims of autonomy and substantive validity as correlates of an *argument of continuity*—which, as we already know, means treating its permanently reinvented *respondere* (notwithstanding the critical interpellation which challenges it) as the pursuit of a project, the cultivating of a *way of life* and the performance of a *tradition*.

4.2 The Articulation Sources/System

How does this approach allows us to experience the sources/system articulation? Let us begin with the last of these two problems, in order precisely to recall that the so-called aspirational perspective (treating law as an order of validity) imposes on the announced *phenomenological–normative* approach (concerning the issue of the sources of law) a dialectical sequence of four moments (Neves 1995, pp. 56–93): *the first one* (*the material moment*) takes into account "the historical–societal reality that provokes the constitution of law" and appears, due to its own diversly structured (natural and social, cultural and spiritual) factors, as "a condition of possibility and emergence, a condition of adequacy and correctness, a condition of relevance and codetermination, and ultimately, for all of this, a condition of positivity and enforcement" of a *certain* Law (Neves 1995, pp. 57–58); *the second one* (*the validity moment*) takes seriously the claim to concretize–perform intentions, aspirations, or materially assumed desiderata (and the community of comparable subjects–persons that gives them a constitutive archetypical sense), while appearing dogmatically assimilated as a context–order of normative principles (Neves 1995, pp. 58–67); *the third moment* (said the *constitutive moment*) assimilates in turn the foundations of validity through a recognizable auctoritas and responds to historical–social reality with an experience of institutional determination or stabilization, the core types of which are evidently custom, legislation, and jurisdiction (pp. 67–90); *the fourth one* (the objectivation moment) guarantees finally that the constituted normative content is effectively integrated into the *corpus iuris* (gives this content a systematical intelligibility), while allowing established law to become a normative–juridically communitarian element and a criterion of juridically relevant practice (pp. 91–93). Even with this rough outline, we can understand the productivity of this scheme and the demanding articulation it justifies, from the outset with regard to the claim attributed *en bloc* to the phenomenological–normative treatment of the issue of sources—namely, that of fully respecting the historical–social specificity (and difference) of the process of constitution–stabilization that contingently takes place in each legal order.

With this specification, the claim at stake gains in fact an unsuspected transparency. We can actually say that considering today, for example, a legal order such as the Portuguese *from the perspective of its constitutive process* does not only mean reconstituting the way this order effectively mobilizes or combines the basic institutionalized types of experience (consuetudinary, legislative, and jurisdictional) or the conditions of equilibrium it fixes or performs, in the context of a civil law tradition, while preserving the legislative type as "its polarizing constitutive mode" (Neves 1995, p. 72): this reconstitution is certainly an indispensable first step, and a complex one, but only a first step. Why a complex one? Certainly because it implies at least thematizing the impact that a certain "change of paradigm"—reinventing the challenges and the configuration of *Rechtsstaat* (while assuming the archetype of *constitutional democracy*)[52]—has in that equilibrium, namely concerning the meaning of constitutionality as such and its (formal or material, "thin" or "thick") sense of autonomy (and self-legitimation) regarding the "standard legislative processes" (Shiner 2005, pp. 115–129).

To highlight this autonomy and its implications gives constitutionality a kind of a border or ambivalent role: first of all, as if we were experiencing the invincible circularity that, not without tensions though, presents the *Constitution* simultaneously as a source of law and as authentic law, while inextricably considering its deliberate loss (or *waiver*) of "flexibility," this one not only as an institutionalized resistance to change (capable of mitigating political–social contingency or political–ideological dependence), but also and most especially as a decisive resource to stabilize or fix the dialectics (the "dualism and equilibrium") between "democracy and rights" (between "public interests" and the "normative content of the fundamental rights," if not directly between politics and law) (Rotolo 2005, pp. 159–160); then also as if, with the consecration of a universally–rationally sustainable mode of patriotism (unequivocally called constitutional patriotism), it were a matter of superimposing (formally or informally) internal and external borders, and thus of generating a no less ambivalent context–horizon of justification—capable on the one hand of disciplining the dialogue between traditions (offering opportunities for reciprocal learning and assimilation, while though imposing insurmountable limits), capable, on the other hand, of legitimizing limits to national sovereignty and the inevitability of a multi–level normative structure, this now inseparable from (although not exclusively produced by) the process and stages of European political integration (Habermas 1998).

The attention paid, in this phenomenological–normative perspective, to the force (or levels of bindingness) attributable to European sources—if not to the role actually performed by EU Law—, gives us the cue to other unavoidable steps, less however to pay attention to other manifestations of a formal legal apparatus operating at the level of international relations, than to go beyond the challenges of statutory Law and its internal binominal dynamics (constitutional/standard legislation, external/internal sovereignty, EU treaties/EU secondary legislation, supranational/national legislation, implementation/standard legislation, self-executing/non-self-executing prescriptions, hard law/soft law) (Rotolo 2005, p. 187).

[52] Rotolo (2005), pp. 159–167 ("*The Change of Paradigm: Contemporary Constitutional Democracies*").

Those steps are in fact expected to discuss the effective connections (still concerning that specific contingent legal order) between statutory law and other types of constitutive experiences (or the changes that give those connections apparently new conformations or demands of equilibrium), as well as the autonomous role (explicitly or implicitly) played by those other types, not only by those that we may say directly institutionalized ones (such as national and international jurisdiction, this one, still regarding EU, as an effective protagonist of an experience of "constitutional pluralism") (Saiz and Solanes Mullor 2025), but also by those, which have an undoubtedly open or diffuse stabilizing process (such as doctrinal dogmatics),[53] without forgetting some constitutive manifestations with an intermediate institutional "nature" (private autonomy, mediation, arbitration) (Shiner 2005, pp. 2–5, 85). The so-called paradigm shift concerning constitutional democracies may in fact still require a final problematization, discussing the impact that, namely on the conformation (if not on the method) of adjudication—justifying, for example, pragmatic–functional models of effectiveness and efficiency, but also more or less intense forms of political–social activism (namely, jurisdictional activism)—the welfarist dimension associated with it may have, at least at the level of the proliferation of *final programs* (this persisting even beyond a strict Welfare State model).

In any case, the thematization announced thus far highlights exclusively the *material moment* and partially the institutional situations of the *constitutive moment*. Following the discussion concerning the relevance of legal doctrine, we could have introduced the thematization of *Juristenrecht* and its more or less decisive contribution to the effective incorporation of legal contents, which is the issue autonomized in the *objectivation moment*: as we all know, doctrinal jurisprudence—through a specific constitutive re-elaboration which is also a heuristic (more or less innovative) anticipation—contributes decisively to giving casuistic *judge-made law* the normative explicitness it needs in order to become authentic *institutionalized law* (at least when it does not benefit from a formally binding case law *stare decisis*).[54] The fruitful intervention of the *moment of validity* generates, however, *qua tale*, a totally different level and a new perspective of problematization, introducing as a limit to a juridically plausible process of positivization the requirement to follow or at least to respect an aspirational dimension.

As it was already highlighted, this is certainly not an ideal, dogmatically closed or a-historical perspective, it is rather a cultural–civilizational conformed and historically situated *constituendo* project-*proicere*, betting on the separability or

[53] *See* exemplarily Peczenik (2007), p. 14 (namely exploring the categories "must-sources," "should-sources," and "may-sources").

[54] There is also the possibility of asking what we should specifically expect today from a successful articulation of jurisdictional and dogmatic jurisprudential practices (with their strong sense of *doing what comes naturally*) as a condition for acknowledging (with Castanheira Neves) that the identity of "communitarian conscience" in terms of its juridical relevance and regardless of the national or transnational stages where we may reconstitute it, depends decisively on these practices and their institutional contexts. This is, however, a door that I will simply leave open here and now. For an attempt to answer this question, see Linhares (2018), pp. 125–127.

autonomy of a certain practical world (instituting the subject–person of comparability and the artifacts that compose this world as a form of life and a tradition), and as such developing, in each context (albeit with the trans-contextual persistence that justifies an *argument of continuity*), a cultural–spiritual mediation between "real" (political, economic, social) factors and other (contextually justified) "cultural (ideological, moral, ethical, aesthetical) factors" (Neves 1975, p. 170). The difference in the reflexive level and the corresponding perspective is, moreover, more drastic than it seems: to include a question directly addressing the *foundations* within the issue of sources of law does not in fact mean simply merging or superimposing questions about sources of knowledge and validity and thus maintaining an *external (albeit moderate) perspective*; only the explicit shift to an *internal normative perspective*, simultaneously defending the compatibility of this *participant point of view* with a *meta-dogmatic thematization* (capable of discussing analogies and differences between institutional situations of diverse contingent orders), allows us to productively understand what is at stake, also realizing that the reconstructed demarcating diagnosis (distinguishing juridically and non-juridical processes of constitution and stabilization) identifies a problem of compatibility between supposedly legal materials that only a methodological approach focused on concrete adjudication (and open to the limiting possibilities of *interpretation according to principles*) can effectively consider and resolve. This conclusion actually opens the door to explore juridically relevant content... and with this the decisive contribution of the questions and answers that the experience of the legal system will make possible.

Whatever the diagnosis that the *phenomenological–normative perspective* allows us to construct—referring to the contingency of a single legal order or to the regularities that are determinable in a more or less vast set of social orders, considering exclusively the present time or reconstructing a shorter or longer temporal process—, the response or the path of response concentrated on the category of intelligibility legal system (illuminated by the same internal perspective) will invariably allow a multidimensional experience, this one constituted by the interaction of five strata or layers: principles, statutes, precedents-exempla, dogmatic models, legal reality. As if the *contents* obtained through various constitutive processes (with different balances between them) were now distributed between *foundational warrants* and *criteria*,[55] all these with unmistakable modes of bindingness or juridical force (and the corresponding presumptions, with diverse methodological implica-

[55] A foundational warrant (*fundamento*) is a *rationale* that gives specific intelligibility or an autonomous sense to a certain field or domain of practice (mainly identifying the commitments that constitute this field): the *rationale* justifies a plausible conclusion, even though it does not propose a solution or a type of solution (i.e., it does not free us from the discursive effort, which is indispensable to reaching the solution). The rule or criterion is an available ("technical") device or apparatus, which can be immediately mobilized ("convened") to resolve a given problem and (or) provides a plausible scheme for finding the corresponding solution (albeit requiring a discursive effort in concretization or realization). The normative principles (extended by some doctrinal models that constitutively specify and reinvent those principles) should be methodologically treated as foundational warrants or rationales. Statutes, judge-made law, and all the other dogmatic models are (or should be assumed as) *criteria*.

tions concerning the construction of concrete adjudication)—with principles (as warrants) benefitting from a presumption of *communitarian validity*, statutes (as criteria) from a presumption of *political–constitutional pedigree* or *authority–potestas*, legal dogmatic models (as warrants or criteria) from a presumption of *rationality* or *rational conclusiveness* and, last but not least, precedents-*exempla* (as criteria) from a singularly contextualized presumption of *correctness* (*justeza, giustezza*)—… or, at the limit, projected onto institutional situations or the canonic experience that constitutes *legal reality* (Neves 1993, p. 154; Bronze 2006, p. 627; Linhares 2012a, p. 58). The contributions resulting from this systemic intelligibility (as a dogmatic-stabilizing dimension indispensable to the *ratio* of concrete adjudication) are indeed decisively clarifying when we project them onto the questions raised by the problem of sources. Or to put it another way, it is actually very productive to *distinguish* between *practices that constitute law* and *practices that stabilize the contents of law* (and as such, to avoid a linear correspondence or an aproblematic continuum between them).

Allow me, to finish, a single example, considering the understanding of normative principles that this systemic intelligibility (and its methodological projections) exemplarily illuminates. If the *phenomenological–normative perspective* allows us to conclude that principles *are not* sources of law, but rather *law tout court*, the meaning of this conclusion gains its full scope when we take seriously the incorporation of principles into the system and when we recognize the diversity of stabilization practices (combining constitutional–statutory, jurisdictional–adjudicative, or dogmatic–doctrinal practices) that shape its content.

Treating principles as *foundational warrants* not only means to break radically with the *continuum* imposed by the category *norm* (even when this continuum, justifying the *norms–rules/norms–principles* binomial, explores a *qualitative* differentiation), but also to free them from the impact of an *indetermination thesis* or an *indetermination generating theory* (Linhares 2017, pp. 92–112, 118–142, 171). This is because we renounce any abstract predetermination of their normative content—arguing that principles provide decisive (argumentative) warrants "*to take up a position* before concrete situations" or "situations which are to be determined concretely"[56]—while simultaneously acknowledging that precisely due to the involved axiological judgment (or to the axiological acquisition that this judgment should reflect), this *taking up of a position* first and foremost claims a discourse of limits (the normative limits of *validity*) whose *negative productive impact* Drucilla Cornell helps us to understand by eloquently describing principles as "lights which come from the lighthouse," essentially guiding us while preventing us "from going in the wrong direction" (Cornell 1992, p. 106).

All this culminates in the acknowledgment that "the true meaning of principles is only determinable in concrete" (Neves 1984, p. 60), which implies arguing that the normative integrity of the *meaning* (and *sense*) of principles demands a

[56] Notwithstanding very different conceptions concerning the sense and roles attributable to principles, Castanheira Neves quotes here expressively Zagrebelski: Neves (1984), pp. 59–60.

well-defined experience, which is simultaneously constitution, manifestation, and performance (a performance which, as a concretizing experiment, always involves a more or less explicit transformation)—and is entirely different from experiences that correspond to statutory, judicial, and doctrinal *criteria* (or the corresponding experiences of autonomization–stabilization). In contrast with principles, all these *criteria* provide plausible *problem–answer schemes* (which is why they should be methodologically treated as *criteria...*) and, as such, anticipate possible problems and situations or situational elements, albeit in different ways (respectively through abstract typification–prevision and programming, concrete exemplification, or reflexive reconstitution).

This reflexive path allows us actually to highlight the specificity of conceiving principles *as ius*—rejecting the common approaches of principles *as ratio* and principles *as intentio*[57]—while dialoguing with a concept of norm that goes beyond norm–*ratio* (and its *Konditionalprogramm*) to include every programming resource available to statutory law (including *Zweck-* and *Relational-programme*)[58]; it allows us, however, mainly to acknowledge an unavoidable practical circularity, involving *on the one hand* the governing normative context offered by principles and *on the other hand* the determining dynamics imposed by problem-solving practices—here as the *novum* introduced by principled realization, i.e., by the practices that follow those principles (and while they follow them). It is as if we were highlighting the dynamics of constitutive historicity, while being aware that the tasks–roles of guiding and guide-following (specifying and transforming, fixing, and developing) permanently interchange and overlap. This means, in fact, considering normative principles both as an axiological (not only regulative but also constitutive) *context* for these practices and simultaneously and inextricably as a normative *correlate* (inferred from the practices themselves). It is as if we were mobilizing two contrary irreducible constitutive forces, the first irradiating from the axiologically relevant presupposition of principles (and their integrating dogmatic *normans*), the second stemming from the irreducible problematic *novum* introduced by practices (and their plural contexts of stabilization and realization).

Unsurprisingly, like many other challenges concerning *practical reasoning*, this has to do with the permanent quest for a specific point of equilibrium, more precisely that which (as a kind of successful, even though always momentary, situated transcendence) recreates a productive dialectical intertwinement between the poles and the contexts or horizons involved (if not an authentic *point of reversibility* between the corresponding terms). It is only when this intertwinement occurs that it seems possible to invoke a full "practical consonance" of *content* between the intentions of performance ascribed to principles (considered as foundational warrants and practical commitments) and the acts of adjudication that follow (perform) these intentions, reinventing them in each case (Neves 1993, pp. 203–204; Linhares 2018, *passim*).

---

[57] *See* supra, note 10.

[58] I am using the well-known formulations by Teubner (1982).

In any case, it is impossible to conclude the exposition of this example without announcing other paths that this conception of principles offers when it comes to exploring the productive relationship between the issue of sources and the issue of the system. Through the distinction *ratio legis/ratio juris* inscribed in the internal experimentation of norms (the first *ratio* considering immanent programmatic teleology, the second the constitutive foundational bond with principles) (Neves 1993, pp. 78–81, 150–157, 188–196 and 278–283)—amplified by other decisive distinctions (between *principles* and *policies* in their well-known general implications, as well as between *contexts of justification and foundation*, this one with regard to the methodologically reflected construction of concrete adjudication) (Dworkin 1986, pp. 206–258, 327–347, and 410–413; Neves 1993, pp. 152–154)—the question to which we return is ultimately the paradigm shift concerning *constitutional democracies*.

As if it were a matter of deciphering the two faces of Janus that *principles as jus*, playing simultaneously as stabilizing practices (specifying normative contents) and as insurmountable limits of validity, cannot help but assume in relation to the political–social institutionalization of the welfarist dimension (or its crisis or its process of overcoming): this double role actually becomes particularly visible (in its inevitability) whenever, diving into a *no man's land* disputed by law and politics, it is precisely a matter of, in the plural context of contemporary legal thinking, exploring the meanings (and the sense) of a *responsibility for solidarity*, if not the guiding idea of *distributive justice*.

5 Conclusions

The conclusion of this journey—which is *long* because of the many doors it half-opens and the crossroads these doors lead to (while allowing us to glimpse a multitude of interlocutors, coming from different times and places), but which is *short* because of the developments it frustrates and the ellipses (if not omissions) with which it protects its implacable dynamic or pace—is, without paradox, the one that this improbable tension between *length* and *brevity* (*complexification* and *simplification*) immediately suggests: the recognition that the mapping of contemporary legal thinking, in its *disconcerting plurality*, gains on the one hand from being taken seriously from an internal perspective (engaged in the radical critical problematization of the Western tradition) and on the other hand from the accurate unveiling of the bonds of separation or overlap that, composing diverse solutions (and opening unexpected experiences of circularity), relate or intertwine (positively or negatively) the transversal issues (the thematic cores) of the sources and of the content of Law (the latter seriously taken in its systemic intelligibility).

With the organization that these two transversal axes allow (in the terms that have been perfunctorily outlined throughout this chapter), the affinities and differences (the *litiges* and *differends*) that feed our present pragmatics of plurality—if not also directly the stage on which this succession of true or false convergences and divergences is vibrantly played out—appear in fact under a new light (or an unexpected lights design), showing precisely that it makes more sense than ever to demand that (in whole or in part) the *Legal "Theory"* that we need today, overcoming without complexes its attributes of theoretical purity or distanced cognitive universality (starting right away with the label of *General Theory* that disfigures it!), take on directly this task of reconstitution and mapping.

This means in fact engaging in an ever-new exercise of experimentation and reformulation of flexible *grids*, which is also, after all, for *Legal Theory*, an interpellation and rewriting of its *memory*—the memory of its lost paradigm, but also, certainly, albeit with less evidence, that of the project or way of life that both the implementation and the overcoming of this paradigm intended (intend?) to ultimately achieve or perform. All this without forgetting that not even here (on a, so to speak, intermediate meta-dogmatic level) does the *argument of continuity* appear in any way protected or immune. Being under the fire of radical problematization (this one questioning the survival of the *form of life* we call Law) is, quite the contrary, one of the conditions of possibility on which this mapping exercise and the "*Theory*" that takes it seriously effectively depend.

References

Austin J (1873) Lectures on jurisprudence or the philosophy of positive law (London 1832), 4th edn. (review and edited by Robert Campbell). John Murray, London

Bergbohm K (1892–1973) Jurisprudenz und Rechtsphilosophie. Kritische Abhandlung, volume I (Leipzig 1892), reprint, Verlag Detlev Auvermann, Glashütten im Taunus

Bierling ER (1965) Zur Kritik der juristischen Grundbegriffe, reimpr. Scientia Verlag Aalen, Teil I, Gotha Aalen

Brockmöller A (1997) Die Entstehung der Rechtstheorie im 19. Jahrhundert in Deutschland. Nomos Verlagsgesellschaft, Baden-Baden

Bronze FJ (2006) Lições de Introdução ao Direito, 2nd edn. Coimbra Editora, Coimbra

Bubner R (1990) Dialektik als Topik. Bausteine zu einer lebensweltlichen Theorie der Rationalität. Suhrkamp Verlag, Frankfurt am Main

Buckel S (2006) Neo-Materialistische Rechtstheorie. In: Buckel, Christensen, Fischer-Lescano (eds) Neue Theorien des Rechts. Lucius & Lucius, Stuttgart, pp 117–137

Coleman J (2001) The practice of principle. In defence of a pragmatist approach to legal theory. Oxford University Press, Oxford

Coleman J (2005) Incorporationism, conventionality, and the practical difference thesis. In: Coleman (ed) Hart's postscript. Essays on the postscript to "the concept of law". Oxford University Press, Oxford

Coleman J (2009) Beyond inclusive legal positivism. Ratio Juris 22(3)

Coleman J (2011) The architecture of jurisprudence—I. The. Yale Law Journal 121(2) http://www.yalelaw journal.org/images/pdfs/1009.pdf

Cornell D (1992) The philosophy of the limit. Routledge, London

Dahm HJ (1994) Positivismusstreit. Die Auseinander-setzungen der Frankfurter Schule mit dem logischen Positivismus, dem amerikanischem Pragmatismus und dem kritischen Rationalismus. Suhrkamp Verlag, Frankfurt

Derrida J (1967) L'écriture et la différence. Éditions du Seuil, Paris

Derrida J (1988) Limited Inc. Northwestern University Press, Evanston

Derrida J (1994) Force de loi. Le fondement mystique de l'autorité. Galilée, Paris
Dubischar R (1983) Einführung in die Rechtstheorie. Wissenschaftliche Buchgesellschaft, Darmstadt
Dworkin R (1986) Law's empire. Harvard University Press, Cambridge
Dworkin R (2006) Justice in robes. Harvard University Press, Cambridge
Dworkin R (2011) Justice for hedgehogs. Harvard University Press, Cambridge
Fikentscher W (1976) Methoden des Rechts in vergleichende Darstellung, vol III. J. C. B. Mohr, Tübingen
Foucault M (1976) L'Histoire de la sexualité, vol I. (La volonté de savoir). Gallimard, Paris
Habermas J (1998) Die postnationale Konstellation. Suhrkamp, Frankfurt am Main
Hart HLA (1994) The concept of law, 2nd edn. Clarendon Press, Oxford
Heidegger M (1985) Vorträge und Aufsätze, 5th edn. Pfullingen, Neske
Jhering RV (1883) Geist des römischen Rechts auf den verschiedenen Stufen seiner Entwicklung, zweiter Teil, zweite Abteilung, 8th edn. Benno Schwabe Co, Basel
Kramer MH (2004) Where law and morality meet. Oxford University Press, Oxford
Linhares JMA (2009) Os desafios-feridas da Allgemeine Rechtslehre. Um tempo de teoria do direito reconhecido (reencontrado?) pela perspectiva de outro tempo de teoria. In: Alves JL et al (eds) Liber Amicorum de José de Sousa e Brito em comemoração do 70° aniversário. Coimbra, Almedina, pp 261–314
Linhares JMA (2012a) Validade comunitária e contextos de realização. Anotações em espelho sobre a concepção jurisprudencialista do sistema. Revista da Faculdade de Direito da Universidade Lusófona do Porto (1):58. http://revistas.ulusofona.pt/index.php/rfdulp/article/view/2966
Linhares JMA (2012b) Na 'coroa de fumo' da teoria dos princípios: poderá um tratamento dos princípios como normas servir-nos de guia? In: Correia A, Machado J, Loureiro J (eds) Estudos em Homenagem ao Prof. Doutor José Joaquim Gomes Canotilho, vol III. Coimbra Editora, Coimbra
Linhares JMA (2013) O direito como mundo prático autónomo: "equívocos" e possibilidades. Relatório com a perspectiva, o tema, os conteúdos programáticos e as opções pedagógicas de um seminário de segundo ciclo em Filosofia do direito. Imprensa da Universidade de Coimbra, Coimbra
Linhares JMA (2016) In defense of a non-positivist separation thesis between law and morality. Rechtsphilosophie Zeitschrift für Grundlagen des Rechts 04:425–443
Linhares JMA (2017) O binómio casos fáceis/casos difíceis e a categoria de inteligibilidade sistema jurídico. Um contraponto indispensável no mapa do discurso jurídico contemporâneo? Imprensa da Universidade de Coimbra, Coimbra
Linhares JMA (2018) The claim for "consonance" between principles and problem-solving practices: the challenge of plurality and the indispensable mediation of Juristenrecht. In: Linhares JMA et al (eds) Jurists' law and European identity. Dogmatic-institutional, methodological and legal-philosophical problems. Instituto Jurídico (UCILeR), Coimbra, pp 107–127
Linhares JMA (2020) Exemplarity as concreteness, or the challenge of institutionalising a productive circle between past and present, old and new. In: Condello A (ed) New rhetorics for contemporary legal discourse. Edinburgh University Press, Edinburgh
Linhares JMA (2025) Translation, Intercultural Dialogue and the Mediation of Legal Semiotics. International Journal for the Semiotics of Law 38: 1463–1481.
Lyotard JF (1983) Le différend. Éditions de Minuit, Paris
Lyotard JF (1990) Pérégrinations. Loi, forme, évènement. Galilée, Paris
Merkel A (1885) Juristische Encyclopädie. Verlag von Guttentag, Berlin
Neves AC (1975) Fontes do direito (II). Boletim da Faculdade de Direito (BFD), LII: 95–240.
Neves AC (1984) O problema actual do direito. Um curso de filosofia do direito, 3th. Version. policop, Coimbra-Lisboa
Neves AC (1993) Metodologia jurídica. Problemas fundamentais. Coimbra Editora, Coimbra

Neves AC (1995) Digesta: escritos acerca do direito, do pensamento jurídico, da sua metodologia e outros, vol 2. Coimbra Editora, Coimbra
Neves AC (2008) Digesta: escritos acerca do direito, do pensamento jurídico, da sua metodologia e outros, vol 3. Coimbra Editora, Coimbra
Peczenik A (2007) Scientia Juris. Legal doctrine as knowledge of law and as a source of law, vol 4. Springer, Dordrecht
Phillips CL (2011) Rescuing Inclusive Legal Positivism from the Charge of Inconsistency. Philosophy Theses, paper 81, http://digitalarchive.gsu.edu/philosophy_theses/81
Postema G (2011) Legal philosophy in the twentieth century: the common law world, vol 11. Springer, Dordrecht
Raz J (2009) Postema on law's autonomy. In: Between authority and interpretation. On the theory of law and practical reason. Oxford University Press, Oxford
Riedel M (1972–1974). Rehabilitierung der praktischen Philosophie. 2 vols. Rombach Verlag, Freiburg
Rotolo A (2005) Sources of law in the civil law. In: Shiner R (2005) Legal institutions and the sources of law (with a contribution by Antonino Rotolo). Springer, Dordrecht
Saiz A, Solanes Mullor J (2025) Constitutional Pluralism
Savigny FCV (1814) Vom Beruf unsrer Zeit für Gesetzgebung und Rechtswissenschaft. Heidelberg
Shapiro SJ (2000) Law, morality, and the guidance of conduct. Legal Theory 6(2):127–170
Shapiro SJ (2009) Was inclusive legal positivism founded on a mistake? Ratio Juris 22(3):326–338
Shapiro SJ (2011) Legality. Harvard University Press, Cambridge
Shiner RA (2005) Legal institutions and the sources of law (with a contribution by Antonino Rotolo) [In A Treatise of legal philosophy and general jurisprudence, vol. 3]. Dordrecht, Springer
Simmonds N (2007) Law as a moral idea. Oxford University Press, Oxford
Stein P (2007) The Roman jurists' conception of law. In: Padovani, Stein (eds) The jurists' philosophy of law from Rome to the seventeenth century, vol 7. Springer, Dordrecht
Teubner G (1982) Reflexives Recht. Entwicklungesmodelle des Rechts in vergleichender Perspektive. Archiv für Rechts- und Sozialphilosophie 68
Waluchow W (1994) Inclusive Legal Positivism. Clarendon Press, Oxford
Waluchow W (2000) Autorithy and the practical difference thesis: A defense of inclusive legal positivism. Legal Theory 6(1):45-81
Waluchow W (2006) Legal Positivism, Inclusive versus Exclusive. In: Craig (ed.), Routledge Encyclopedia of Philosophy, http://www.rep.routledge.com.libaccess.lib.mcmaster.ca/article/T064
Welsch W (1991) Unsere postmoderne Moderne. Acta Humaniora, Weinheim

José Manuel Aroso Linhares Full Professor (Professor Catedrático) of *Legal Theory and Philosophy of Law* at the *Faculty of Law* of the *University of Coimbra* and at the Lusófona University (Portugal). He has been, during several years, the Coordinator of *UCILeR* (the University of Coimbra Institute for Legal Research) and the Vice-President of *Associação Portuguesa de Teoria do Direito, Filosofia do Direito e Filosofia Social*, the Portuguese Section of IVR.

Uncertitudes and Unpredictabilities in the Legal System: The Application of the Law Under Discussion

Pierre Moor

Abstract The legal system is seen as a means of regulating social behavior; to fulfil this function, its essential quality must be stability, so that its reactions to what is happening in society —both in relations between individuals and between the state and the governed—are predictable. To this end, there is a principle, that of the legal security, by virtue of which legal subject must be able to rely on the stability and predictability of the law. But it is not always possible; the configuration of the factual situations require often that a space of liberty in the application of the law has to be given to the authority, creating uncertainty on the solution it will be chosen finally. The text considers the problems they are set thus on sight of the principle of the predictability.

1 Introduction

1.1 Problems of Method

1.1.1 The Question of Uncertainty in the Legal System

The legal system is seen as a means of regulating social behavior; to fulfil this function, its essential quality must be stability, so that its reactions to what is happening in society —both in relations between individuals and between the state and the governed—are predictable. To this end, there is a principle, that of the legal security, by virtue of which legal subject must be able to rely on the stability and predictability of the law.

P. Moor (✉)
University of Lausanne, Centre of Public Law, Lausanne, Switzerland
e-mail: pierre.moor@citycable.ch

E. C. B. Bittar (ed.), *General Theory of Law*,
https://doi.org/10.1007/978-3-032-22517-7_4

However, practice shows that there are crucial moments in the legal process when uncertainty reigns: the establishment of facts (what are the facts that prompted the judge to take action?), the interpretation of texts (what do they mean?), and their application (how does their meaning qualify concrete cases?). If there were not so often uncertainty as to what the law—i.e., the judge—[1] will say about what is brought before him, there would be no need for lawyers, legal proceedings, or judges: it would be enough to read the texts and deduce the expected answer!

The purpose of this contribution is to analyze the causes of these uncertainties and the ways in which the law has instituted to remedy them. To say what the law really has to say—and what it must say—since it is obliged to rule as soon as it is seized of a question, it must remove the uncertainties and transform them into certainties; otherwise, the conflicts it must settle could not be resolved definitively: as the proverb says, only the fool builds his house on sand.

1.1.2 Analysis Tools

These analyses come under the heading of *Theory of Law*: insofar as it reflects on legal practices, it explains them in order to better understand the structure of the system to which they belong. The starting point is a basic axiom, which appears to be a banal observation: the law is designed to be applied to the conflicts it addresses, to put an end to them. The entire legal system is structured to implement this purpose in a manner that is coherent and accessible to reason.

From this perspective, the legal proceedings can be broken down into several phases. The first is the transmutation of factual situations, whose reality is initially merely invoked, into proven facts, which then form the factual basis for the application of the law: this is the establishment of so-called "relevant" facts. The second is the clarification of the general meaning of the legal norms to be applied, which is by no means always clear: this is the interpretation. The third is that of application: do the factual circumstances of the case to be decided—circumstances defined in the first phase—fall within the scope of the legal norms as interpreted in the second phase? The final point, where, in this third phase, the law is pronounced, is then reached, in a binary logic of alternatives: either the law applies, or it does not.

This decomposition is not a set of legal assertions and therefore does not resort to legal concepts; on the contrary, it takes legal concepts as its object of reflection. From this perspective, *Theory of Law* is not a mere legal discipline, but a *Social Science Epistemology*. As we will be relying on the contributions in the following pages, it may be useful to briefly outline the *Theory of Law* used here.

The *Theory of Law* can thus highlight the fact that the legal system is a system of actors who contribute to its implementation: legislators, judges, lawyers, legal advisors, law school professors—the whole corporation of jurists—to whom must be

[1] We use the terms "judge" or "authority" to designate any state body competent to take binding decisions in specific cases, i.e., a judicial body or an administrative authority.

added the individuals and persons to whom the system confers the status of legal subjects and treats them as such. *Systems theory*[2] enables us to understand the functioning of this set of actors as a whole.

The work of the system is accomplished through a specific language. In other words, law has a linguistic dimension[3] as an essential element: it functions through the exchange of texts, whether oral or written. These texts are made up of sets of *signs*, which is why we turn to *Semiology* to describe the modalities of these exchanges, in particular by using the structure of signs as it has brought it to light[4]: a *sign* is made up of a *signifier* (*significant*, fr.)—for law, the lexicon and syntax of ordinary language—and a *signified* (*signifié*, fr.), which is the meaning assigned to it by the legal code; the *referent* (*référent*, fr.) is the thing about which the *sign* is used. So the text of the norm (or /cat/) is the *signifier* (*significant*, fr.), the meaning assigned to it by the legal code (or "little domestic feline") is the *signified* (*signifié*, fr.), and the norm itself, as created by the adoption of a text (or the cat referred to in the sentence "the cat is outside, lying on the mat"), is the *referent* (*référent*, fr.).[5]

1.2 Causes of Legal Unpredictability

The uncertainties that give rise to unpredictability in the application of the law are not caused by imperfections in the drafting of texts or in the logic of their application, although for a long time the latter was supposed to follow the model of the *syllogism*—the so-called *judicial syllogism*—according to which any concrete meaning of the law should always be already contained in a preexisting valid abstract norm (at least in continental law). Although this model turned out to be a utopia that judicial practice never achieved, it remains in the legal unconscious as an ideal to be attained as far as possible, to approach—always as far as possible—the predictability of the law, or in other words, to ensure the security of legal relationships.

In fact, the uncertainties of the law have a completely different cause. They stem from the unpredictability of the factual situations with which the law is going to be confronted,[6] and with which the judge, who must resolve the disputes submitted to him and is obliged to do so—the law implies a constraint to respond as soon as a case is referred to him[7]: he cannot apply to himself the maxim *in dubio abstine*, on

[2] Inspired by Edgar Morin, in his book (1977).

[3] Moor (2021), p. 31 ff, 47 ff. Ricœur (1986): « condition langagière » (p. 62).

[4] We are referring here to the semiotic triangle, as conceptualized by Ferdinand de Saussure in his *Cours de linguistique générale* (2002).

[5] Moor (2010), p. 71 ff, et (2021), p. 47 ff.

[6] Today, given the extension of the State's remit, there is a real difficulty in legislating, i.e., drafting legal texts: cf. Moor (2016), p. 79 ff.

[7] On the response constraint and its implications, see Moor (2005), pp. 144 ff, and (2010), pp. 114 ff, 291 ff.

pain of committing a denial of justice, which the legal order represses. It must therefore transform uncertainties into certainties.

It should be noted that the temptation to overregulate does not appear to be an adequate means of resolving the problem. We can apply to law what Hamlet says about *Philosophy*: "There are more things in heaven and earth, Horatio, than are dreamt of in our philosophy." Overregulation fails to provide for everything: can we even imagine everything that would have to be provided for to eliminate the uncertainty associated with determining what adequate causality might be in any given case of liability? It would be an enormous list, and the more precise it is intended to be, the more gaps will appear in its future application.

The normative edifice (the legal order) must therefore enable the judge to work out a solution in a situation of uncertainty about which the law gives only general indications, leaving him a certain freedom of choice. In other words, abstractions whose openness is such that they are capable of absorbing in advance an indeterminate infinity of concrete cases, despite their unforeseeable diversity. To take the example of adequate causality—a central concept in tort law—the jurist has only a general and open definition: an event is the adequate cause of a result "when, according to the ordinary course of things and the general experience of life, it is proper in itself to bring about a result of the kind that has occurred."[8] Hence, the unpredictability of the application of law.

It is the task of *Theory of Law* to reveal the argumentative paths the judge follows in applying the law, and to transform uncertainty into the certainty posed by the judgment he delivers: *res judicata pro veritate accipitur*. We will accompany the judge along his or her path, from the moment a case is referred to him or her to the decision that brings the proceedings to an end, in order to shed light on how and at what cost uncertainties are removed, while respecting the requirement for rationality, which is essential to the rule of law system and must be achieved in any application of the law.

Indeed, this requirement is fundamental.[9] In these states, for any assertion to qualify as a legal norm, be it general or particular, it is not enough for an authority with jurisdiction to adopt it; it must also, and even more so, be justified by an argumentation that is likely to establish its validity from the point of view of reason, i.e., it must be motivated in the course of the legal proceedings that formally legitimizes it. The corollary of this requirement is the need to publish the grounds that justify the act to be decided. This dual requirement will be present throughout the text that follows.

---

[8] Definition adopted by the Swiss Federal Court, for example in its decision ATF 123 III 112. All the judgments cited here as examples have been published in the Swiss Federal Supreme Court's collection of judgments (hereinafter ATF) and are also available at https://www.bger.chjurisprudencearretsprincipaux.

[9] See Moor (2010), pp. 166 ff., (2016), pp. 155 ff.

1.3 Uncertainties in Legal Work

This process begins with the selection of the facts that will determine the application of the appropriate standard for resolving the legal question at the origin of the legal action: the so-called "relevant facts" (ch. 2.1). However, these facts are not immediately given to the judge in their reality, but only "established" (as jurists say) with the help of *clues*[10] that are likely—or not—to prove their reality: are these *clues* sufficient for us to consider that the reality of the facts of which they are in some way the markers is proven (chap. 2.2)? Finally, is the *normative program* (*programme normatif*) outlined by the standard sufficiently precise to allow us, by simple deduction, to logically base the solution to the question posed without any hesitation—given the frequency of indeterminate notions contained in legal standards, which will lead us to distinguish between their interpretation and their application (chapters 3.2 and 3)? All these operations must be argued (ch. 4), in order to establish their rationality convincingly and open up the application of the law to guarantees against judicial arbitrariness (ch. 5).

At each of these moments, from the start of the construction of the judgment, there is a state of uncertainty that the data available to the judge does not allow him to decide in a logically predictable way: the judge hesitates[11] between several possible solutions—between several *narratives* (*récits*) joining together what he knows into the most coherent whole possible, to give the best possible account of what he is going to decide: this mode of research is called in logical terms *abduction*.[12] Only when the construction is complete is the uncertainty lifted. But this is only the case in the special semantic and epistemological universe of law: it is therefore relative, produced by an argumentation that aims to convince with the persuasive force of abductive argumentation (ch. 4). To be acceptable, this relativity requires guarantees, which are those offered by the rule of law (ch. 5).

These states of uncertainty are inherent with the semantic and epistemological universe: this is why the law needs jurists: some—the lawyers—present their own abductive argumentations, others—the judges—decide definitively on the basis of theirs. And it is for this reason, too, that it is not enough to read the texts—legal or jurisprudential—to predict with certainty how the law will be applied. As for the

---

[10] The Italian historian Carlo Ginzburg (1986) has brought into light for the first time the indicial logic as a new paradigm, pp. 158. See his deconstruction of the narrative constructed with clues by the police and the judge to establish the reality of a fact—the presence of the accused on the place of the crime (1991).

[11] On the predominance of this sentiment among judges, cf. Latour (2004), pp. 104, 153/4, 161/2, 181, 187, 202.

[12] Cf. Eco (1988), p. 49 ff, (1992), pp. 253 ff, p. 272. Let us remember that abduction consists, in the absence of certainty about the existence of a fact, in formulating a hypothesis (a narrative) from a set of clues in order to draw the most likely conclusion. For readers unfamiliar with this concept, a trivial example: "the grains of rice on my plate are white," "the grains of rice in this bag next to me are all white," "I can abduce that the ones on my plate come from this bag." Abduction is the process of the Ginzburg indiciary logic (see n. 10).

litigants (*litigants* in French is *justiciables*: note the passive connotation of this term!): they await the solutions to which these arguments will succeed. This concept of waiting (or expectation; *Erwartung*, ger.), highlighted by Niklas Luhmann,[13] is the other side of uncertainty: waiting for the solution to be given by the judge. Previously, the expectation of one of the parties is opposed to that of the other, and the judge must decide.

1.4 The Function of the Moments of Uncertainty

1.4.1 The Law, Between Repetition and Imagination

Uncertainty is not only inherent with the legal universe: it is an essential factor in it. And demonstrating this is the very purpose of *Theory of Law*. For it is uncertainty that enables the judge to consider the concrete circumstances of the cases submitted to him. It is also what enables him to import social knowledge, customs, and ethical conceptions into his argumentations, thus giving them a basis in law. It makes legal work not only an enterprise of repetition, repeating what has already been decided, but also of imagination, in the discovery and innovative use of grounds for decision taken from the social universe of which he is a member. The judge is at once a function and an individual person: what we have called a figure of the legal order,[14] like a Janus who can see both, through one of his faces the legal universe and through the other the social universe to which he belongs.

This original combination of memory and imagination is necessary to open the law to its environment, provided it is integrated into a system that offers guarantees against both the rigidity of repetition dictated by memory and the excesses of the imagination.

1.4.2 A Few Words on Predictive Justice

What do artificial intelligence (AI) tools bring to the problem of legal uncertainty? We can illustrate the problems they are likely to cause by briefly presenting the example of *predictive justice*, a concept that has emerged in the United States in recent years. It involves "the analysis of all available case law, by an algorithm, and the use of the history of judged litigation to predict the potential outcome of future trial."[15] Without going into the substance of the debate that this creation of artificial intelligence provokes, it should be noted here that, while it leads to a greater *verisi-*

[13] Luhmann (1995), especially pp. 131 ff, and on the temporal dimension, ibid. especially p. 124. Cf. Moor (2021), p. 142.

[14] Cf. Moor (2016), pp. 204 ff.

[15] Definition given by Arens 2018 (original French text). See also the fact sheet published on jurisguide.fr.

militude (*vraisemblance*, fr.) of the outcome of the trial envisaged, it does not eliminate uncertainty in its very principle, like any prediction (except those of Cassandra, who were not believed!). On the other hand, it does not indicate the reasons why a particular motive is retained, nor the weightings between these motives, with the result that any debate on the rationality of the prognosis is excluded. In other words, by achieving *verisimilitude* (*vraisemblance*, fr.), *predictive justice* does nothing more than produce an abduction, i.e., what the judge does, as we shall show, but without having to justify the argumentation that led to it. It therefore favors the work of *repetition*, by means of the considerable information it makes available. And it renders the current guarantees ineffective, since the work of weighing up the reasons for the solution is invisible.

2 Uncertainty About the Law Itself

2.1 *The Principle of Legal Security*

Uncertainty seems paradoxical in legal systems where the principle of security of the law is paramount: the law must be predictable. It is even the very foundation of the principle of legality. The *European Court of Human Rights* expresses this explicitly when it defines the law, in relation to the principle of legality: "A norm cannot be regarded as a 'law' unless it is formulated with sufficient precision to enable the citizen to regulate his conduct: he must be able—if need be with appropriate advice—to foresee, to a degree that is reasonable in the circumstances, the consequences which a given action may entail."[16]

But we shall show that uncertainties during legal operations are dictated by the nature of things: it is not possible to formulate texts in which everything that could happen in their field of application would be foreseen, where all the concreteness of present and future "things in the world"[17] would be absorbed by abstract notions.

2.2 *Case Law Reversals: Legislative Changes*

However, we can point to two configurations in which unpredictability exists within the legal order itself.

If there is one event that is by its very nature unpredictable, it is a reversal of jurisprudence: the abandonment of a well-established jurisprudence or practice on

[16] *Sunday Times v. United Kingdom* (no. 1), 26.4.1979, Series A, vol. 30, § 49). Note the caution of this definition, marked by the mention of "appropriate advice" and "at a reasonable [...] degree."

[17] To quote Greimas (1976), pp. 84 ff.

the interpretation or application of a norm to change its meaning. Only specialists can guess at its possibility, by decoding the motivations of precedents.

Jurisprudence imposes several constraints on reversals, of which we will mention just one: they must be justified. The judge must set out the reasons justifying the change.[18] And it is immediately applicable to the case in question, even if it is to the detriment of the litigant who brought the matter before the court, who would have benefited from the abandoned case law—the only one he knew. This is to avoid a paradoxical situation: if the judge recognizes that the previous case law can no longer stand, it is because he considers that it is not or no longer in conformity with the legal order, and that it would therefore be contradictory to apply it as soon as this recognition is made. The fact remains, however, that the principle of legal certainty is subject to uncertainty: a reversal is always possible.

The same applies when an authority decides to change the norm it has adopted: the principle is that no one has the right to maintain the law. If it were otherwise, if everyone could demand to remain subject to a law that had been repealed on the grounds that the situation giving rise to the application of the law predated the adoption of the new law, the result would be great chaos in the legal order, which would no longer be applicable to all equally, which would be contrary to the very concept of law.

In both situations, it is as if there were constant unpredictability, permanent uncertainty as to the stability of the legal order, justified by the political need to enable the openness and dynamism of the legal system, and thus its adaptability to social, ideological, ecological, and economic mutations.

3 Uncertainty About the Facts

3.1 Determining "Relevant" Facts

One of the parties to a dispute brings a case before a judge. He claims that a norm of the legal order gives him a right against the other party—the defendant—and invokes a factual situation which, in his opinion, corresponds to the conditions to which the text of the norm subordinates its application.

We deliberately use the term "factual situation" here: at this stage, we are dealing with the various circumstances involved in the universe of "the things in the world," not all of which are of interest in judging the case. It is therefore necessary to sort through them to bring out the "facts"—which are said to be "relevant," i.e., the referents of the topical *signs* of the normative text. In this case, it is the interpretation

[18] See the example given and note 27.

of the norm that brings out its normative program: what this norm has to say about the dispute in question, which *referents* are "relevant." The first uncertainty arises when the normative density of the normative text is more or less explicit on this point—we will come back to this point below (ch. 4.1).

3.2 *The Proofs*

However, these facts are rarely immediately given: their existence in the reality of the "world of things" must be established. There are, of course, situations in which proof is given without the need for any further investigation—for example, civil status data as recorded in an official register, or a breathalyzer reading. When proof must be provided, the general rule is that it must be supplied by the person claiming a right: this is the burden of proof (*onus probandi*).[19]

Most of the time, the judge only has *clues* of the reality of the fact: they must be sufficiently probative: what does this mean? The judge has to put forward a hypothesis that brings them together in a narrative that he considers sufficiently plausible for him to accept the fact as proven: an evidential narrative. It is a process known in logic as abduction: it does not lead to certainty, but rather to conviction. Once the judge has ruled, the fact is considered established or not: *res judicata pro veritate habitur.*[20] This conviction—the intimate conviction of the judge, as the jurists say—must not only be that of the one who decides (the judge), but must be sufficiently strong to be likely to meet with the overall approval of any reasonable (who can be referred to as his acceptance, i.e., the ability of the narrative pro acceptance, i.e., the ability of the probatory narrative to be read as convincing by a collectivity, the potentially universal audience, to use a concept due to Chaïm Perelman—we will come back to this later).

However, two situations of particular configuration should be noted. The first is where, generally speaking, it is nearly impossible for the party bearing the burden of proof to provide it. In this kind of situation, the legislator institutes a presumption, either irrebuttable (it cannot be overturned) or rebuttable (the burden of proof to the contrary lies with the opposing party—for example, in paternity proceedings). The other situation is where it is materially impossible to provide proof, but the law requires that the fact be established—for example, two people, who are potential heirs to each other, die in the same disaster, leaving no survivors who

---

[19] The legal system may, however, provide that the judge may himself order investigative measures.

[20] The principle dates back to Roman law; it is found in the *Digest* (D. 44, 2,6), citing the jurist consult Paul (160–230). The possibility of revision must be reserved, as a legal way open if evidence is discovered that could not previously have been known.

could testify: the law must then establish a fiction (so, the older person died first, therefore his or her property is included in the estate of the other).

As we can see, the law is not concerned with the entire factual situation that gave rise to the dispute, but only with some of the events that occurred there. Those that are normatively relevant and, moreover, are accepted as proven. This means that there is always some degree of uncertainty as to the actual existence of the factual basis on which the law is applied.

4 Uncertainty in Questions of Law

4.1 *Normative Density*

The law manifests itself in texts (laws, judgments, contracts), written in the common language. It therefore has a linguistic dimension: it uses words—in semiotic terms, *signs* (*signes*, fr.). But these *signs* (*signes*, fr.)[21] have varying degrees of precision, which do not always allow us to deduce their meaning in concrete cases; in legal jargon, they are said to have varying *normative density* (*densité normative*, fr.).

Normative density (*densité normative*, fr.) is the degree to which the *terms* of the norm make it possible to deduce their meaning in concrete cases.[22] It is exhaustive when the standard contains numerical data fixing a maximum or minimum, as in the content of a certain substance in a type of food, or when it refers to civil status data recorded in an official register (as in dates of birth): no operation other than a simple deduction is necessary for application to a given individual. It is weak when application to a concrete case requires entire argumentation to determine whether it is a case, or a non-case of the term used in the norm. In *Semiology*, we would say that the "thing of the world" may or may not be considered as a referent of the normative sign, which may or may not therefore receive legal qualification. In such configurations, these terms are referred to as indeterminate legal notions.

The determinate notions do not pose any problems either in terms of interpretation (with a few exceptions, cf. below) or in terms of their practical application: no uncertainty. The same cannot be said of indeterminate concepts, even if their meaning in everyday language is clear: for example, what is a "forest" in a standard that prohibits land clearance: what surface area, what place in the landscape, what ecological or protective function, what tree species must characterize a specific shrubby grouping to qualify as a "forest" within the meaning of the law? Paradoxically, such concepts are central to the law: fault, adequate causality,[23] just cause, for example;

[21] See above ch. 1.1.2.

[22] See Moor (2010), pp. 117 ff, et (2021), pp. 66 ff.

[23] See note 5.

even in the field of fundamental rights (personal freedom, public interest, proportionality).

4.2 Legal Interpretation

Interpretation may be required even for specific notions: for example, should a given term be understood as epicene? Or is the starting date of a time limit for appeals, set by law as the day the decision is received by its addressee: the day of receipt or the following day? Uncertainty remains until a competent authority has given the meaning that, in its interpretation, the law should have. And even if, following this interpretation, practice is established on a continuous basis, there is nothing to exclude a reversal of jurisprudence, in consideration of other motives, which a new case brings to light.[24]

The situation is more complicated for indeterminate concepts. To apply them correctly, it is first necessary to be clear about the meaning of the norm: in other words, to interpret the normative text whose adoption by the competent body was intended to create it, an interpretation that will lead to the identification of the *normative program* (*programme normatif*, fr.): this will contain guidelines, an enumeration of the criteria to be applied, the delimitation of the goals to be pursued, and indications of the weightings to be applied. In the application phase, these various guidelines provide only limited certainty: while they can be used to censure a concrete decision that omits one of the criteria they mention or introduces a criterion that is foreign to the normative program, uncertainty remains as to which criterion will be applied. However, as we shall see below, there is still uncertainty as to their respective weights, which can only be assessed in the light of the concrete circumstances of individual cases.

4.3 Applying the Law

It is not for lack of care in the conception and drafting of normative texts that the legislator inscribes indeterminate legal notions.[25] The diversity and originality of "things in the world" are such that it is impossible to foresee them all in their idiosyncrasy in order to formulate them in general and abstract texts; it is therefore necessary to resort to notions whose indeterminacy enables them to subsume all the circumstances that, in the future, are likely to correspond to the aim pursued by the norm. Imagine the legislator trying to transcribe into determinate notions all the circumstances that might constitute "fault" in the law of civil liability; or everything

[24] On case law reversals, cf. Moor (2010), p. 250 ff.

[25] See Moor (2016), pp. 79 ss.

that might be qualified as a "religious act" to be guaranteed by freedom of religion: turbans, daggers, wigs, beards, pendants, veils, pants, food, and so on—the human imagination is infinite, leading to uncertainty not only as to the qualification of this or that "commandment" as a "religious act," but also as to the regime of restrictions that, from the angle of the public interest—one of the most indeterminate notions there is—may be imposed on it.[26]

It is true, as we have said earlier, that indeterminate notions do in any case have a normative program that gives indications, which are criteria for their concretization. However, these criteria do not all have the same importance (some may only be subsidiary), but above all they may lead to different conclusions, hence the need to weigh them in order to arrive at an answer. In other words, as the major of the syllogism is insufficient to enable him to decide the case, the judge must develop a minor of syllogism—for example, "for Sikhs, wearing a turban is a religious act," "for Jews, not working on Saturday is a religious act," "for Muslims, nubile women must cover their hair," or "the surgeon who performs an operation after consuming alcohol is committing an offence," "wooded areas with such and such characteristics are forests," and so on. These minors constitute particular norms, in relation to the general norm, of which they are the specification required to be able to decide the case as a case of the general norm.[27] On the basis of this minor standard, which is new to the existing legal system, and only after having elaborated it, can the judge conclude: "this woodland grouping has these characteristics, therefore it is a forest, and therefore it cannot be cleared."

The methodological problem is to move from the major to the minor. If, in some cases, this passage is obvious (e.g., in the case of the surgeon cited above), in a majority of cases, an argument is needed to justify it ("is compliance with a dress code laid down by a religious text a religious act?" with regard to the constitutional guarantee of freedom of conscience and belief). However, if an argumentation is necessary, this also means that another argumentation would be possible, leading to another solution. Once again, there is a moment of uncertainty before the judge chooses between the possible arguments. In this sense, in this type of configuration, the act of judging is an act that can be described as micropolitical, because the adoption of the minor poses a new norm, since it was still unknown before its elaboration—that is, unknown in the legal order before its adoption.[28]

Finally, in most cases of uncertainty, it is the analysis of the concrete case in all its idiosyncrasy, in all its individuality, as presented to the judge, that makes it possible to decide. The assessment of the respective weight of the various criteria that can be abstractly derived from the *normative program* (*programme normatif*, fr.)

---

[26] On this point, see Moor (2021), pp. 183 ss. Compare two *Swiss Federal Court* rulings on whether or not to grant exemptions from mixed school swimming lessons for girls or boys: ATF 119 (1993) I a 178 (an exemption must be granted; this concerned a girl), and 135 (2009) I 79 (it must not; in this second ruling, the exemption had been requested for boys).

[27] On this point, see Moor (2010), pp. 261 ff.

[28] Cf. Moor (2010), pp. 298 ff. and (2021), in particular pp. 67, 70, 86, 93 ff.

depends on the contingent individuality of the case. However, it is precisely to enable this concrete judgment that the legislator uses notions with a low normative density: he cannot further determine, through abstractions, all the situations that might arise in the application of the norm he is drafting.

5 Argumentation

5.1 Argumentation by Abduction

No jurist can do without the experience of argumentation.[29] As explained above, argumentation is required at every stage of the legal proceedings: in the interpretation of the applicable norm, in the identification of the facts that are relevant to the application of the norm, in the selection of the modes of proof required to establish the facts, in deciding whether the evidence adduced is sufficient to demonstrate the facts, and, finally, in the application of indeterminate legal concepts or in the definition of determinate ones. Consequently, many moments when, before a decision is made, uncertainty reigns: what will the decision be, when there is nothing to predict it deductively from the applicable general standard?

All argumentation is constituted as a chain of motifs and forms a *narrative* (*récit*, fr.), whose characters would be abstractions—like allegories. The links between the motifs as a whole are formed by successive abductions—abductions, because there is no logical necessity governing the passage of motifs from one to another. What's more, these links can be built by different abductive paths and lead to other possible *narratives* (*récits*, fr.). The most plausible abductions will prevail as the judgment is built up.

But what does *verisimilitude* (*vraisemblance*, fr.) mean?[30] The judge must obey a double programming,[31] when hesitating and will therefore *choose* on the basis of his competence to apply the law—which implies a margin of freedom. This double programming results from the legal order: on the one hand, the *normative program* (*programme normatif*, fr.) of the legal norm that gives him this margin, and on the other, the standards of general application, such as the principles of proportionality, good faith, or the prohibition of arbitrariness. The second results from the status of his function within the community of which he is a member, and in whose eyes, he must make his decision convincing enough to be acceptable, if not accepted. In his argumentation, he uses the motives that correspond to the mores, customs, values, knowledge, experiences, and conceptions that seem vernacular to him. Here, we encounter the judge as a figure of the legal order: he looks at both sides of the programming.

[29] Cf. Moor (2016), pp. 145 ff.

[30] See Moor (2021), pp. 225 ff.

[31] Moor (2021), pp. 72, 95, 213.

5.2 Examples of Double Programming

Some examples of this double programming will help to clarify our approach.

For decades, the text applicable to the divorce in Switzerland of foreign spouses was interpreted as requiring that the divorce be recognized by the state of origin and, if the spouses were of different nationalities, by both states. In 1968, the *Swiss Federal Supreme Court* reversed its position[32] and modified the interpretation of the applicable text, defining the requirement differently: it was now sufficient for the *plaintiff* spouse's country of origin to recognize the Swiss judgment. Extract from the motives: "If the judge cannot base himself on considerations relating to the desirable law, he must nevertheless endeavor to apply the law in a way that is as consistent as possible with the current situation and mentality. To this end, he will often be led to abandon a traditional interpretation, which was undoubtedly justified when the law was drawn up, but which is no longer tenable because of changed circumstances or even the evolution of ideas. [...] The cumulative application of the national laws of each of the two spouses can only be defended by openly stating the principle that divorce must remain an exceptional means of dissolving a marriage. Such an assertion is irreconcilable with reality, both in Switzerland and in most neighboring countries." It should be added that, in this case, the husband, who was the defendant, was Italian and that Italy, at the time, did not sanction divorce, which allowed Italian husbands to cheat on their French wives with total impunity—this being the marital situation the Tribunal had to judge. It is interesting to note that the judgment was delivered by a five-judge court, by a majority of three to two.

Another example is also perfectly illustrative.[33] At a time when political rights in Switzerland were reserved for men, the *Federal Court* had to rule on the extension of political rights to women, but only in one of the Swiss cantons, the one in which the appellants were domiciled. They argued that, in the relevant texts, the word "Swiss"[34] was epicene and therefore refer not exclusively to Swiss men; they asserted that there was no objective and relevant difference justifying the discrimination, and that a non-epicene reading therefore violated the principle of equal treatment. The judge opted for a historical interpretation: the texts in question dated from the second third of the nineteenth century and, from their adoption until the time of the judgment (1957), had been continuously read as they had originally been conceived. What made him choose this argument rested on another consideration: if, on the basis of their argument, he had granted the appellants the right to vote they were seeking in the canton where they lived, this would have implied that male-only suffrage, as practiced at federal level and in all other cantons, would also have to be

[32] ATF 94 (1968) II 65.

[33] ATF 83 (1957) I 73.

[34] In French, German, and Italian (the three official languages in Switzerland), the lexicon uses two different terms to distinguish the two sexes: « Suisses » and « Suissesses », « Schweizer » and « Schweizerin », « Svizzero » and « Svizzera ». At the time of the ruling, the constitutional text said only « Suisse », « Schweizer », and « Svizzero ».

recognized as unconstitutional. According to the judge, such an upheaval could not be decided by a court, even a supreme court, but had to be decided by the constituent body itself; consequently, it was out of the question for the applicable texts to be interpreted by it according to contemporary conceptions, in an epicene reading. This was despite the fact that, as in the previous example, all the surrounding states had already adopted women's suffrage. In this case, it was likely that acceptance of the appeal would hardly have been compatible with political conceptions of the distribution of powers as they were current in Switzerland, and that its acceptance was therefore not sufficiently broad. This was not the case a few years later, when the *Federal Supreme Court* imposed women's suffrage on the last of the federated states to resist it, all the others and the Confederation itself having introduced it in the meantime.[35]

Consider also the commotion caused by the ruling that allowed a husband to have his marriage annulled on the grounds that his wife was not a virgin, which he had noticed on the wedding night. The appeal court overturned this ruling, redefining the notion of "essential quality," the absence of which in the *French Civil Code* justifies the annulment of a marriage.[36]

5.3 Acceptance and the Universal Audience

In these examples, argumentation does not aim to impose itself logically: it seeks to convince, and its persuasiveness—and therefore its *acceptance*, its aptitude to convince—depends on its *verisimilitude* (*vraisemblance*, fr.). But to whom is it addressed? In principle, first and foremost, the parties to the case: but it is only natural that the losing party remains convinced that the argumentation he or she presented to defend his case was the right one. Then to the legal profession, mainly legal doctrine, which, in its review of jurisprudence, will approve or criticize the arguments,[37] and to other authorities. Finally, to the community at large, for whom the norm is intended to serve as a model of behavior.

This indeterminate whole can be brought back to the concept of the *universal audience* (*auditoire universel*, fr.), highlighted by Chaïm Perelman.[38]

We can also highlight a differentiation within the concept of imperativeness; *institutional imperativeness*, which derives from the arrangement of competences, whereby what has been judged and is no longer subject to appeal, is definitive and

---

[35] ATF 116 (1990) I a 359.

[36] See the newspaper *Le Monde*, May 29, 2008, and November 19, 2008.

[37] For example, criticizing the Federal Court, in its decision allowing a Muslim father to obtain an exemption from his nubile daughter's compulsory swimming lessons (ATF 119 [1993] Ia 178), for not rejecting the Muslim's appeal on the grounds of the constitutional principle of gender equality; the Federal Court reversed this ruling in a subsequent decision (ATF 135 [2009] I 79), based essentially on considerations of integration of the foreign population resident in Switzerland.

[38] Perelman/Olbrechts-Tyteca (1958), pp. 40 ff; Perelman (1984), p. 95. Cf. Moor (2021), p. 227 ff.

can no longer be contested through the legal channels—*res judicata pro veritate habetur*, as we have already said—and *epistemic imperativeness*, which is relative, in the sense that any judgment can be criticized on its merits, but without any effect on what has been judged—this is why the Latin locution formulates this rule cautiously: it does not say that the thing judged *is* the truth but *has to be accepted* as being the truth.

Uncertainties are thus lifted, to become institutional certainties, although their validity remains open to criticism. This is what makes the system dynamic and constantly open to its environment, both legal and social, instead of being closed in on itself.

6 Warranties

6.1 Constitutional Guarantees

For this arrangement to function effectively, it needs guarantees, which were introduced as early as the nineteenth century in the course of the political evolution that established the rule of law. They are interwoven one with the others.

First, the writing down of the law and the publicity of justice, so that its decisions can be read and circulated freely as information on the models of behavior imposed by the State. It is by putting things down in writing that the author can realize the coherence of what, before, he only thought.

Second, the obligation of the authorities to give the reasons for their decisions, so that the reader, whoever he or she may be, understands why this or that abduction has been retained.[39]

Third, the independence of the judiciary—otherwise, the rule of the judge's personal conviction would be meaningless.

Finally, freedom of opinion, so that decisions can be discussed and even challenged—even if such challenges (mainly by legal doctrine) have no other effect than to open up debate.

All these constitutional guarantees are part of a fundamental principle of the rule of law: that any act of public authority, from the adoption of a law to its application, must have a reasonable basis. We have called this principle the *general requirement of rationality* (*exigence générale de rationalité*, fr.).[40] It also means that the realiza-

[39] The *European Court of Human Rights* has ruled that the obligation to state reasons is one of the guarantees of Article 6 ECHR. The truth is, however, that this obligation is implemented very differently from one country to another: for a long time, it was very imperfect, for example in France (see Pascale Deumier [2018], pp. 67 ff), while it is often very abundant in countries with a Germanic tradition. On this obligation in general, see Fanny Malhière (2013) and Frédéric Géa (2007). On the practical application of this approach, see the thematic dossier published by Alain Lacabarats (2022).

[40] Moor (2010), pp. 166 ff., (2021), pp. 98, 229 ff.

tion of this requirement, whatever the act it is supposed to justify, must be open to discussion: this is what these guarantees, which are in their essence profoundly democratic, are also intended to achieve.

6.2 Sociopolitical Guarantees

We have referred to *Semiology* to understand how legal texts work. However, this work of decoding that each jurist carries out daily does not take place alone in an ivory tower: jurists are constantly talking, listening, reading and writing to each other, each in a specific role, a specific function. In other words: their corporation is a system of actors, and, by the same token, the law must also be described as such, and not just as a set of norms, which, existing only on paper (and increasingly today, in computer memories), require the work of this system of actors to be effective.

By system, following Edgar Morin,[41] we mean a set of elements, all of which belong to the whole by participating in its functioning, and none of which has any full meaning outside this belonging. The legislator would be nothing without a judicial system to apply his laws, and judges would be deprived of the instruments necessary for their function, and without the specific training they have received from doctrine. Finally, the latter must be understood as the environment in which all the legal material produced by the legislature and the courts is analyzed, classified, and sorted.

This system must therefore function in such a way that it respects, or better still, implements the constitutional guarantees essential to the sociopolitical effectiveness of corporate justice. More specifically, it must ensure correspondence with what is happening in civil society: that the gaze it casts on civil society, composed as it is of the figures of the legal order, provides it with the information it needs to keep in step with it, and can send it messages, in the form of special norms, which it receives and must be able to understand.

This implies sociopolitical uses in the functioning of the social structures of the actor system.

This applies as well to the legislator, but this is ensured by the structure of the elected parliament given to him by the constitution. However, this structure must be sufficiently defined by the legislator to eliminate any risk of electoral fraud. We might add that the financing of political parties must be transparent, to avoid private economic forces endowing them with different financial resources, distorting their electoral competition.

The same applies to the judiciary. The election of judges must respect the ideological relations existing in society. Their election procedure must not depend on periodically changing political majorities. Their independence must not be

[41] Morin (1977), especially p. 94 ff.

compromised by the risk of not being reelected if they do not follow the ideologies of the parties that put them forward for election.

Finally, access to the legal profession must be financially open to all classes of the population.

We can see that the legal system, made up of the normative system and the system of actors in charge of it, cannot function in isolation: it must be both closed by the normative apparatus it produces, and open to the society from which it emanates. This is made possible by the duality of the figures of the legal order, as well as by the uncertainties of the law, in which lie the possibilities of this Janus gaze, opening the perspective of double programming.

7 Conclusions

We have shown the legal situations in which the normative edifice leaves uncertainties as to its application, uncertainties that are only lifted by a judge's decision, unforeseeable for the litigants since it only comes at the end of the procedure. Litigants, if they have "enlightened advice,"[42] can only rely on degrees of *verisimilitude* (*vraisemblance*, fr.)—just as judges can only decide on the basis of an assessment of likelihood, i.e., on the basis of abduction.

We have also shown that such situations are consubstantial with the law. To establish facts, judges have only *clues* (*indices*, fr.) at their disposal. As far as the law is concerned, the linguistic formulation (and there can be no other) of legal texts, which use abstractions, cannot grasp the full diversity of the "things in the world": these abstractions can only be concretized by reference to the idiosyncrasies of individual cases, or to the ethical, scientific, economic, or ecological conceptions circulating in their environment: in this way, legal abstractions are filled with a substance of external origin, which, by becoming part of the arguments used to justify the decision, becomes the grounds for the decision and is thus "legalized": an exchange of information, as the law sends out to its sociopolitical environment the message of the new norm that has been elaborated within it to specify the indeterminate legal notion. An argumentative imagination is needed to fill the gaps left by references to the knowledge accumulated in memory, knowledge that is not sufficient to make a decision.

So, on the one hand, decisions are adapted to reality and their environment, and on the other hand, they are adapted to legal order insofar as argumentation can be integrated into the normative program of the applicable standard: it is the double programming (*double programmation*, fr.). Finally, there is a democratic basis, since the standards have been adopted in a parliamentary procedure or, if delegated, by law.

[42] In the words of the *European Court of Human Rights*, quoted above.

Situations of a priori uncertainty are not only consubstantial with the legal system, but they are also necessary for it to keep pace with society—one responding to the other, and vice versa. This means that innovations in the normative system are not only a matter for the legislator, but also for the judge when it comes to resolving uncertainty. As a result, the work of the judiciary itself has a political dimension, insofar as the judge introduces a new norm into the normative system, through the solution that removes the uncertainty. This operation is due to the material necessity that the law finds itself in, more frequently than is generally thought, to take on the idiosyncrasy of the case it has to decide, which is not comparable to any other in all the diversity of "things in the world," and therefore unforeseeable in its concrete existence.

While these unpredictabilities can be useful, and even necessary, both to justice and to the effectiveness of the law, they also carry a considerable risk of arbitrariness—as shown by the laws of totalitarian states (in the interpretation, for example, of the notions of "security of the State" or "good morals").[43] This is why they must be integrated into the legal system of states governed by the rule of law, so that effective control can be exercised over their resolution.

References

Arens Ch (22 octobre 2018) Compte rendu du colloque sur la « Justice prédictive : évolution, révolution ? [archive] », sur Cour d'appel de Paris. https://www.cours-appel.justice.fr/paris/compte-rendu-du-colloque-sur-la-justice-predictive-evolution-revolution. Consulted in 03.05.2025

Deumier P (2018) Attendu que la phrase unique est progressivement abandonnée. Revue trimestrielle de droit civil:67

Eco U (1988) Sémiotique et philosophie du langage. Trad. Myriem Bouzaher. PUF, Paris

Eco U (1992) Les limites de l'interprétation. Trad. Myriem Bouzaher. Grasset, Paris

Géa F (2007) Contribution à la théorie de l'interprétation jurisprudentielle : droit du travail et théorie du droit dans la perspective du dialogisme. LGDJ, Clermont-Ferrand

Ginzburg C (1986) Miti, emblemi, spie. Einaudi, Torino

Ginzburg C (1991) Il giudice e lo storico. Einaudi, Torino

Greimas A J (1976) Analyse sémiotique d'un discours juridique. In: Greimas A. J. (éd.) Sémiotique et Sciences Sociales. Seuil, Paris, p. 84 ss

Lacabarats A (2022) La motivation des décisions de justice. Principes et illustrations dans l'espace judiciaire francophone. Publications des Cours judiciaires suprêmes francophones. https://www.ahjucaf.org/sites/default/files/2022-05/Motivation%20des%20décisions%20de%20justice%20Alain%20Lacabarats%20MAJ%20mai%202022_0.pdf. Consulted in 03.05.2025

Latour B (2004) La fabrique du droit : une ethnographie du Conseil d'État. La Découverte, Paris

Luhmann N (1995) Das Recht der Gesellschaft. Suhrkamp, Francfort s./M

Malhière F (2013) La brièveté des décisions de justice (Cour de cassation, Conseil d'Etat, Conseil constitutionnel): Contribution à l'étude des représentations de la justice. Dalloz, Paris

Moor P (2005) Pour une théorie micropolitique du droit, Paris, PUF

[43] To cite an example provided by Olivier Jouanjan and cited in Moor (2010), p. 192 ff., the interpretation given to the notion of "good morals," under the Nazi regime, to declare a sales contract between a Jewish merchant and a German buyer null and void.

Moor P (2010) Dynamique du système juridique. L.G.D.J, Genève/Bruxelles/Paris, Schulthess/Bruylant/
Moor P (2016) Perméabilités du système juridique. Presses de l'Université Laval, Québec
Moor P (2021) Le travail du droit. Presses de l'Université Laval, Québec
Moor P, Flückiger A, Martenet V (2012) Droit administratif I: les fondements. Berne, Stämpfli
Morin E (1977) La Méthode I: La Nature de la Nature. Seuil, Paris
Perelman C (1984) Le raisonnable et le déraisonnable en droit. L.G.D.J, Paris
Perelman C, Olbrechts-Tyteca L (1958) Traité de l'argumentation. P.U.F, Paris
Ricœur P (1986) Du texte à l'action: essais d'herméneutique II. Le Seuil, Paris
de Saussure F (2002) Cours de Linguistique Générale. Le Seuil, Paris

Pierre Moor Honorary Professor at the *University of Lausanne* (Switzerland). He is *Emeritus Professor* at the *University of Lausanne* and *Doctor H.C.* at the *University of Basel.* He is the author of a three-volume treatise on administrative law (the latest edition in collaboration with coauthors) and works on legal theory.

MIX
Papier aus verantwortungsvollen Quellen
Paper from responsible sources
FSC® C105338

If you have any concerns about our products,
you can contact us on
ProductSafety@springernature.com

In case Publisher is established outside the EU,
the EU authorized representative is:
Springer Nature Customer Service Center GmbH
Europaplatz 3, 69115 Heidelberg, Germany

Printed by Libri Plureos GmbH
in Hamburg, Germany